PROFESSIONAL DEVELOPMENT GUIDE

CARING & ENGAGING SCHOOLS

Partnering with Family and Community to Unlock
the Potential of High School Students in Poverty

ESSIE B. HILL
Frisco, Texas

Copyright ©2019 by Essie B. Hill, Ed.D. All rights reserved.

Published by Essie Hill, ActuateDevelopmentCompany
5729 Lebanon Road, Suite 144229
Frisco, Texas 75034
www.actuatedevelopment.com

No part of this publication may be reproduced, stored in a retrieval system, or transmitted in any form or by any means, electronic, mechanical, photocopying, recording, scanning, or otherwise, except as permitted under the 1976 United States Copyright Act, without the prior written permission of the Publisher, except in brief passages for review purposes. Send permission requests to info@actuatedevelopment.com.

Cover Design: Beau Morrow and Ken Small
Book design: Ken Small
Author photo: Mohammad Dezfuli

Includes bibliographic references

Library of Congress Control Number: 2019910550
ISBN: 978-1-7320021-2-8 (paperback)
    1. Public Education, Secondary—professional learning
    2. School Improvement

Printed and bound in the United States of America
FIRST EDITION

Contents

Introduction: How To Use This Guide..2
Part I: The Struggle With Educational Inequity..5
Chapter 1: My Starting Point: Northwood High School..7
Chapter 2: What Is The "Marriage Of True Minds"?...11
Chapter 3: Results Of A Dysfunctional Marriage Of True Minds............................14
Chapter 4: What Poverty Looks Like In High School: Loss Of Hope.......................17
Chapter 5: What Poverty Looks Like In High School: Disengagement....................20
Chapter 6: What Poverty Looks Like In High School: Impaired Well-Being...........26
Part II: Synergy Toward A Solution..29
Chapter 7: Restarting: Beyond Failed Tradition..31
Chapter 8: The Caring & Engaging Schools Model..34
Chapter 9: Interrelated Mindsets That Reengage Students: Hope.............................42
Chapter 10: Interrelated Mindsets That Reengage Students: Growth.......................45
Chapter 11: Interrelated Mindsets That Reengage Students: Sense Of Purpose........49
Chapters 12-14: Talent Development Program: Self-Regulated Learning,
    Tapping Into Talents, And Embedded Learning..54
Chapters 15-16: The Context Of Well-Being: School-Based Mental
    Healthcare To Benefit All Students & Building A School-Based
    Mental Health Program..57
Chapters 17-18: The Context Of Socioeconomic Integration: School
    Desegregation To Benefit All Students & Surmounting Barriers To
    Socioeconomic Integration...63
Chapter 19: Making Systemic Reform Happen...67
Chapter 20: The Stage Is Set For The Players...70
Appendix: Strengths-Based, Whole-Child Teaching Practices
    To Promote Equity And Social Justice For Economically
    Disadvantaged High School Students..75
Appendix References..95

INTRODUCTION
HOW TO USE THIS GUIDE

I am so excited about my book *Caring & Engaging Schools: Partnering with Family and Community to Unlock the Potential of High School Students in Poverty* and this companion *Professional Development Guide*. The guide can be an effective tool to help educators examine a strengths-based, whole-child education approach, recognizing the perspective as a best teaching practice. Learning will promote a teacher's own self-awareness and will include strategies to engage economically disadvantaged high school students (and all students) in learning, as well as support student development and build relationships.

Educators can use the guide after reading the book or finishing each chapter. They may use *Caring & Engaging Schools* and its companion development guide as content for book study, small group discussion, or professional learning community. Also, an educator can work on his own or consider working with a colleague.

The guide contains learner-centered professional development organized around individual reflection and purposeful collaborative problem-solving activities. A leader is not required, but it may be helpful to have roles such as facilitator, coordinator, notetaker, etc. to engage in various activities.

Organization of the Guide

Part I of the guide is called "The Struggle with Educational Inequity." In this section educators will review barriers to learning from the perspective of disadvantaged high school students and impaired or neglected relationships among the school, family, and community that have contributed to the problem. Learning experiences are designed to help educators become more self-aware of their own experiences or knowledge of the challenges associated with teaching low-performing high school students living in poverty.

Part II is entitled "Synergy Toward a Solution." Educators

will explore ideas and strategies that advance educational equity for all students, especially students living in poverty. Educators engage in learning designed to support a strengths-based, whole-child education reform characteristic of caring and engaging schools, building a foundation for students' school and lifelong success.

Rather than cover all aspects of the book, the guide is intended to address specific ideas that might warrant further consideration. In some cases, chapters will be combined into one learning and development section, particularly those with similar ideas. Each chapter study begins with a brief introduction or review of chapter contents and is presented in the following format:

Thinking it Through: In this section educators individually reflect upon the topics and issues related to the themes of Parts I and II. The intent is to help teachers develop greater self-understanding and awareness about instructional practices and work-related responsibilities, enabling them to recognize areas of strengths and areas for improvement in order to become more effective. Educators contemplate experiences, knowledge, and beliefs in order to deepen their understanding about the learning challenges of low-income struggling high school students and arrive at new understandings associated with how educators' existing expertise and practices fit into strengths-based, whole-child teaching and learning practices.

Extension Group Activity for Further Thought and Discussion: This part requires educators to extend their thoughts through group activities and conversations designed to generate resources, strategies, and new perspectives, supporting strengths-based, whole school reform and student success. Group divisions and activity timeframes may be adapted to fit the needs of the learning community.

The Takeaway: In this section educators individually will write 2-3 key points or insights gained from reading, reflecting on, and/or discussing the main ideas in each chapter. Points or insights may include those things a teacher learned about herself (as related to the teaching and learning process) that she did not know.

An **Appendix** is included at the end of the *Professional Development Guide*. It contains a set of teaching practices and action steps for implementing a strengths-based, whole-child education approach to promote an equitable and socially just education for economically disadvantaged high school students. The strategies benefit youth from all socioeconomic backgrounds.

PART I: THE STRUGGLE WITH EDUCATIONAL INEQUITY

Key Points

- The desperate struggle to reach lower-income students is impacted by their mitigating life conditions that weaken their schooling outcomes—factors that place them at an educational disadvantage.
- Income inequality in society has already placed some high schoolers at an educational or aspirational disadvantage.
- Students from low-income families comprise the majority of the lowest-performing students in our public schools.
- Low-income students come to school with different needs than their middle-class and more affluent peers—needing extra academic help, alleviation of poverty stressors, and help with behavior issues. They also lack the benefits their wealthier peers have (e.g., enriching out-of-school activities, logistical and emotional support at home).
- Education reform measures have been put in place to raise the achievement of low-income students, but we have yet to level the playing field for disadvantaged students.
- Education inequity is education that is unfair and socially unjust. School programs and resource allocation can contribute to unequal and inequitable educational performance, results, and outcomes because they are structured and allocated in ways that may be unfair for economically disadvantaged students.
- Under-resourced students will remain so, unless schools and society actively work together to improve students' conditions.
- Inequities harm not only students living in poverty but also threaten to derail U.S. economic growth and development.

References

Glossary of Education Reform. (2016). "Equity." Great Schools Partnership. Retrieved from https://www.edglossary.org/equity/

Reardon, Sean (2011). "The widening academic achievement gap between the rich and the poor: New evidence and possible explanations." In R. Murnane & G. Duncan (Eds.), *Whither Opportunity? Rising Inequality and the Uncertain Life Chances of Low-Income Children*. New York: Russell Sage Foundation Press.

Suitts, Steve (2015). *A New Majority: Low Income Students Now a Majority in the Nation's Public Schools*. Southern Education Foundation. Retrieved from http://www.southerneducation.org/Our-Strategies/Research-and-Publications/New-Majority-Diverse-Majority-Report-Series/A-New-Majority-2015-UpdateLow-Income-Students-Now

Chapter 1

My Starting Point: Northwood High School

Unfortunately, far too many of the students in high poverty schools like Northwood High School (a pseudonym; see Preface of *Caring & Engaging Schools*) are unprepared to transition successfully to college or other postsecondary education and careers because they lack foundational knowledge and skills. Moreover, students are not attaining proficiency on high stakes tests—all of which are factors indicating educational inequity. In this chapter, you will explore the role assessments play in achieving educational equity, become more aware of the differences between educational inequity and inequality, and understand the reason equity must be an educator's ultimate goal in providing instruction.

THINKING IT THROUGH

Choose one or more of the individual reflection topics below to stimulate inquiry for deepening awareness and understanding.

1. Do assessment practices in your classroom or school contribute to educational equity for students living in poverty, or do practices intensify the challenges students already face? Please explain.

2. Formative assessments should be used as powerful tools to meet teachers' data needs to improve learning and achievement. To what extent do the assessment practices in your classroom or your school promote learning and improvement?

3. How can changes be made on district and state assessments to ensure schools are providing a quality education for all students?

_____
_____
_____

4. Is Northwood High School similar to or different from the school or schools with which you have worked? If so, please describe.

_____
_____
_____

EXTENSION GROUP ACTIVITY FOR FURTHER THOUGHT AND DISCUSSION
Education Inequity vs. Education Inequality

Education inequity and education inequality are oftentimes used in similar contexts and are used interchangeably, but they have different meanings and contribute to different outcomes.

- Working with your colleagues (in pairs or triads), identify the differences and similarities between educational inequity and educational inequality. As you brainstorm, feel free to use online and other resources to help you complete the chart.

- Consider these points in your comparison: definitions of each, 2-3 examples or situations indicating each, impacts of each on students' educational and life outcomes, impacts on the U.S. (social, economic, political, etc.).

- Write the differences of each in the corresponding outside circles; similarities or connections between the two should be placed in the middle section (the circle overlap). Use the Venn Diagram on page 9.

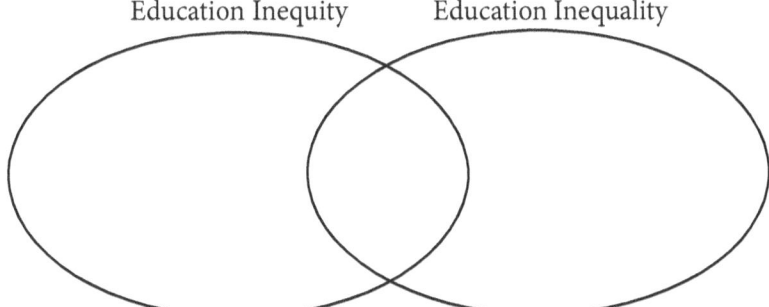

- At the end of 15 minutes, come together as a whole group to discuss your responses. Transfer the Venn Diagram to a white board or large piece of chart paper to record information.
- Include responses to the following in your discussion:
  - Why is it important to know the difference between educational inequity and educational inequality?
  - Why must educators prioritize equity as the ultimate goal? Consider this: Students living in poverty usually come to school lagging academically behind their higher income peers because of out-of-school factors beyond the school's control. Will giving them the same resources as their higher income peers create equity or the quality education they need to succeed? Please explain.

References

U.S. Department of Education (2017). EVERY STUDENT SUCCEEDS ACT Assessments under Title I, Part A & Title I, Part B: Summary of Final Regulations. Retrieved from https://www2.ed.gov/policy/elsec/leg/essa/essaassessmentfactsheet1207.pdf

U.S. Department of Education, Office of Elementary and Secondary Education (2018). *Understanding the Every Student Succeeds Act: A Parents' Guide to the Nation's Landmark Education Law*. Washington, D.C.

THE TAKEAWAY

In the space below, write 2-3 key points or insights you gained from reading, reflecting on, and/or discussing the main ideas in Chapter 1.

1. _____
   _____
2. _____
   _____
3. _____
   _____

Chapter 2

What is the "Marriage of True Minds"?

The content in this chapter explores the "marriage of true minds" metaphor to help educators focus on the key players in the high school ecosystem: administrators, teachers, students, parents, and the broader community. Educators will take a closer look at how poverty and school/family/community relationships impact students' education and life outcomes.

THINKING IT THROUGH

Choose one or more of the individual reflection topics below to stimulate inquiry for deepening awareness and understanding.

1. Do you think the school, family, and community relationship at your school is like a "marriage of true minds"? Why or why not?

   _____
   _____
   _____

2. How do the school/family/community relationships impact student learning and achievement at your school?

   _____
   _____
   _____

3. Have you worked at schools experiencing challenging relationships with parents from low socioeconomic backgrounds and/or with low-income communities? How can the gap among the school, family, and community in these environments be bridged?

   _____
   _____
   _____

4. How would you describe the relationships you have with the parents/families of the students you teach? Do you believe the relationships affect student performance?

_____
_____
_____

EXTENSION GROUP ACTIVITY FOR FURTHER THOUGHT AND DISCUSSION
Round Robin Discussion

Read and/or review Chapter 2 before meeting with your learning group. Write 4-5 ideas from the chapter that appealed to you or caught your attention.

- Divide into groups of 3-5. Each group should have a notetaker and coordinator to help keep group members on track. Group members sit in a circle to begin the discussion.
- The discussion begins when one member of each group shares one idea with the other members of his or her group. The group member begins the discussion with one of the following phrases: "I now understand," "I learned," or "I realized." Avoid using evaluative phrases like "I believe," "I think," "I feel," etc.
- When the first group member is done speaking, the group member to his or her left either adds to the first group member's statement or begins a new understanding, learning, or realization statement.
- Discussion continues in this manner until every group member has spoken at least twice.
- When the conversation has concluded, debrief with this question: How will understandings, learnings, and realizations impact your teaching practices?
- The notetaker records a summary of the discussion and provides other group members with a copy of the information.

THE TAKEAWAY

In the space below, write 2-3 key points or insights you gained from reading, reflecting on, and/or discussing the main ideas in Chapter 2.

1. _____
   _____
2. _____
   _____
3. _____
   _____

Chapter 3

Results of a Dysfunctional Marriage of True Minds

The dysfunctional marriage and community support that often exemplifies the school/family/community relationship has in part contributed to our failure to address effectively a quality or equitable education for high school youth in poverty. Learning in this chapter consists of digging deeper into how beliefs, experiences, and impaired or neglected relationship among the partners in this group has contributed to the underachievement of many low-income high school students. Relatedly, educators will also explore the causes of dysfunctional or poor teacher-student relationships.

THINKING IT THROUGH

Choose one or more of the individual reflection topics below to stimulate inquiry for deepening awareness and understanding.

1. To what extent do you think the challenges low-income high school students experience academically is a result of a dysfunctional relationship among the school, family, and community?

   _____
   _____
   _____

2. To what extent has the belief that low-income high school students are incapable of the high academic performance leading to success affected educators' instructional practices to prepare students for postsecondary education and careers? What evidence do you have that low-income students can think and perform at higher academic levels?

   _____
   _____
   _____

3. As an educator, have you ever witnessed students who gave up on schooling because of a poor academic self-image? How did you feel? How were your relationships with students affected?

_____
_____
_____

4. Do stronger school/family/community networks to support positive student development matter? Please explain.

_____
_____
_____

EXTENSION GROUP ACTIVITY FOR FURTHER THOUGHT AND DISCUSSION
Gallery Walk: Causes of Dysfunctional Teacher-Student Relationships

Relationships are at the heart of the teaching and learning process. Of specific importance is the relationship between the teacher and the student, as the relationship affects student learning and engagement.

- As a group, brainstorm what you perceive to be causes of dysfunctional or poor teacher-student relationships (consider all students but focus especially on teacher relationships with low-income students). Limit causes to 4-5. Write each one in the center of separate pieces of large white poster paper; use a marker to draw a circle or square around each cause. (Using markers with this activity will work well.)

- Set up stations or posters around the room, on the walls, or on tables. Space each around the room to reduce crowding. Each person walks to each station to write comments, thoughts, reflections, or comments about others' written ideas.

- When the writing stops, participants take a gallery walk on their own, with a partner, or in small groups.

Each participant records impressions or takes informal notes while walking from station to station. Remember to disperse throughout the room to decrease clusters around stations.

- Then come together as a group to debrief prevailing thoughts, discoveries, and conclusions. End with or include a conversation about this question: How do you build strong teacher-student relationships? You may consider having a notetaker record debrief information and then send it out to the whole group via email, etc.

Reference

"Gallery Walk" (2019). Retrieved from https://www.facinghistory.org/resource-library/teaching-strategies/gallery-walk

THE TAKEAWAY

In the space below, write 2-3 key points or insights you gained from reading, reflecting on, and/or discussing the main ideas in Chapter 3.

1. _____

2. _____

3. _____

Chapter 4

What Poverty Looks Like in High School: Loss of Hope

In this study you will explore how loss of hope—one of the major stumbling blocks of schooling for disadvantaged high school youth—contributes to educational inequity. The primary focus is about under-resourced students whose hope mindsets need wholesale development rather than enhancement. Loss of hope impacts not only students' ability to fully engage in the productive learning that empowers them to transition successfully to adulthood and fulfill potential but also impacts educators' efforts to provide effectively a quality education.

THINKING IT THROUGH

Choose one or more of the individual reflection topics below to stimulate inquiry for deepening awareness and understanding.

1. What is loss of hope? Reflecting upon what you know about students living in poverty, what are some of the root causes of loss of hope? (Consider in- and out-of-school contexts that may affect in-school or academic success.)

   _____
   _____

2. How does loss of hope impact disadvantaged high schoolers' ability to engage effectively in learning?

   _____
   _____

3. Why is it important to resurrect students' hope? In your response consider how hope is linked to these concepts: motivation, self-efficacy, and goal setting.

   _____
   _____

4. How is a deficit of hope associated with behavioral and emotional challenges? How do behavioral and emotional challenges affect students' school success?

_____
_____
_____

EXTENSION GROUP ACTIVITY FOR FURTHER THOUGHT AND DISCUSSION
Fishbowl Activity

To deepen your understanding of Chapter 4, read the poem "Dreams" by Langston Hughes. (Due to copyright laws, the poem is not included but can be accessed on the web at https://poets.org/poem/dreams). Then engage in a fishbowl discussion with colleagues. Divide the group into two equal groups (Group 1 and Group 2) to form an inner and outer circle.

> **Topic:** Hughes uses images of a "broken-winged bird" and a "barren field" in his poem "Dreams" to illustrate the importance of holding on to dreams. Dreams are the things you hope for or the goals you want to achieve. Using the poem (and its meaning) as a reference, discuss the following:
> - How is academic learning and success connected to dreams and hope? How do academic struggles or failures affect having dreams (or holding on to dreams) and students' sense of hopelessness?
> - In what ways have the impaired or neglected relationships among the school, family, and community (perhaps unknowingly) contributed to disadvantaged high school students' loss of hope?
> - What are some of the consequences for economically disadvantaged high school students if they give up or fail to hold on to hope?

- Members of Group 1 sit in chairs, forming an inner circle, or "fishbowl" to discuss the topic above by sharing their opinions and asking questions of members in their group, if necessary. Group 2 members sit in chairs around Group 1 members, forming an outer circle. Remaining quiet, Group 2 members listen carefully, observe, and take notes of the discussion taking place in the fishbowl.

- After 10 minutes, the members of Group 2 go to the inner circle to discuss the topic, while the members of Group 1 go to the outer circle and remain quiet. Group 2 members discuss the topic, each member sharing his or her opinion and carrying the discussion deeper and further, while Group 1 members listen carefully, observe, and take notes.

- After 10 minutes, the two groups intermingle, talking together to debrief; this may be done in pairs or triads. They reflect on what they learned from the discussion about hope and dreams, including 1) having conversation about how students' sense of hopelessness impacts educators' attempts to provide effectively an equitable/quality education and 2) discussing ways the impaired or neglected school/family/community relationships affect students' loss of hope (e.g., academic struggle and expectancy for a better future).

Reference
"Fishbowl." Retrieved from https://www.unicef.org/knowl edge-exchange/files/Fishbowl_production.pdf

THE TAKEAWAY
In the space below, write 2-3 key points or insights you gained from reading, reflecting on, and/or discussing the main ideas in Chapter 4.

1. _____
   _____
2. _____
   _____
3. _____
   _____

Chapter 5

What Poverty Looks Like in High School: Disengagement

Disengagement from schooling is another stumbling block impeding the achievement of under-resourced high schoolers. In addition to looking into the role impaired or neglected relationships among the school/family/community play in this equation, teachers will examine the connection among poverty, disengagement, and cognitive development.

THINKING IT THROUGH

Choose one or more of the individual reflection topics below to stimulate inquiry for deepening awareness and understanding.

1. How can we address the disengagement problem that is so prevalent among disadvantaged high schoolers?

   _____

2. What can be done to offset poverty's effect on students' cognitive development?

   _____

3. To what degree do you think parents of high schoolers decrease their engagement or fail to support their teens' education because of the belief that students are mature enough to handle the education process on their own?

   _____

4. In high schools where you have worked, how was the school/community partnership bridged to help all students engage in schooling, helping them succeed in the transition to adult roles?

_____
_____
_____

EXTENSION GROUP ACTIVITY FOR FURTHER THOUGHT AND DISCUSSION
Mind Maps Exercise

This exercise is designed to deepen your understanding of how living in poverty may impair students' socioemotional wellbeing, reducing academic performance and preparation for life.

- Divide into 4 equal groups: 1, 2, 3, and 4. Each group creates a mind map to provide an overview of the main or central idea of one of the passages below (continued on pages 22-25) from Chapter 5, pages 41-44 of *Caring & Engaging Schools*. (To review bibliographic information for the passages, see the Endnotes section of the book.)

- Use a large white piece of paper to create the mind map. Put the central or main idea of your passage in the center of the map, and then create branches (extending in all directions) of related ideas. You can also create sub-branches from main branches to expand on ideas and concepts. Use colors, images, diagrams, sketches, etc. to represent words, ideas, and issues.

- At the end of 25 minutes, each group presents mind maps to the whole group, providing explanations, summaries, and insights.

Reference

"Enhance Student Study Activities with Mind Mapping." (2017). Retrieved from https://www.qualitymatters.org/qa-resources/resource-center/articles-resources/mind-maps

Group 1 Passage

POVERTY'S EFFECTS UPON COGNITIVE DEVELOPMENT

Neuroscience, sociology, and learning theory have converged upon a powerful link between poverty and cognitive development. Living in poverty contributes damaging effects upon the developing brain, compromising the child's ability to function cognitively and hence to learn, which tends to reduce academic achievement.[16] Biology therefore provides a key reason that children in poverty lag behind their more affluent peers, beginning before preschool and continuing throughout the elementary, middle, and high school years.[17] Poverty stressors thus both limit the social development of cognitive skills and hamper the brain's critical growth and maturation.

Economically disadvantaged students thus are more likely to experience numerous cognitive problems that interfere with learning: short attention spans, difficulty keeping focused, struggles with generating new solutions to problems, and trouble monitoring the quality of their work. If available mental resources are inadequate for the task, the learner struggles to interpret and apply ideas and information; engaging in true learning is made unnecessarily challenging.

The multiple harsh direct or indirect stressors associated with poverty all compromise young people's cognitive development. In particular, the prefrontal cortex, the brain region most affected by childhood growth and stress—as well as adolescence's spurt of psychosocial and physiological change—is affected. The prefrontal cortex, in charge of such broad functions as personality and social behavior, also largely controls the specific "executive functions" (self-regulation, self-monitoring, and working memory) that are requisite for focusing on learning.[18]

Group 2 Passage

Executive Function Impairment

The executive functions are necessary not only for academic achievement and workforce success, but also for maintaining close relationships, raising children, and generally getting along with others in the world. Along the developmental journey from infancy to adulthood, executive functioning is refined continuously, as individuals learn and adapt cognitive skills while exposed to increasingly complicated and challenging tasks. In other words, executive functions are not innate, but acquired and built.

Executive functioning may be compared to the air traffic control system at a busy airport. Just as the tower manages multiple planes landing on and taking off from many runways simultaneously to avoid crashes, the well-developed human brain learns to perform complex coordination of ideas, motivations, and priorities.[19] Executive functioning enables youth and adults alike to manage all the streams of information we receive and create, so we can plan projects, see them through, and adjust when situations change. For students to engage in goal-directed or problem solving behaviors, they have to prioritize, organize, delay gratification, follow rules, react to events as they unfold, and cope with frustration.

The executive function skills are generally viewed as three basic dimensions: working memory, inhibitory control, and cognitive flexibility. Working memory holds information in the mind while it is manipulated and used in reasoning. Inhibitory control is the self-regulatory skills used to restrain impulses, filter distracting thoughts, resist temptations, pause and think before taking action, maintain focus, and prioritize actions. Cognitive flexibility is the ability to self-monitor—to switch gears and adjust to changes in plans, demands, or viewpoints; to re-establish overall priorities; to change strategies in response to feedback; and to apply skills or rules in their appropriate settings.[20]

Group 3 Passage

Executive Function Impairment (Continued)

Clearly, the executive functions directly affect how well students manage school and succeed academically.[21] Students are asked to plan and manage so that they finish schoolwork on time, pay attention to and remember details, evaluate ideas and reflect on their work, and ask for help or seek more information when needed. Although youth coping with learning or attentional disabilities, behavior disorders, traumatic brain injury, or autism are regularly associated in the schools with deficits, students without diagnosable disabilities also experience impairments of or periodic struggles with executive functioning.[22] The latter are disproportionately low-income students, for whom the multiple stressors of living in poverty have chronically undermined the healthy development of executive functions.[23] Children from economically disadvantaged backgrounds experience significantly greater levels of environmental and psychological stressors: exposure to physical and verbal violence, family turmoil, untreated substance abuse or mental illness, inadequate nutrition, financial worry, environmental toxins, and low cognitive stimulation at home (e.g., not being read to, and being engaged in less complex and meaningful conversation). Is low cognitive stimulation a stressor or a result of stress?

The resulting cognitive problems of low-income students may manifest as difficulties in planning projects, communicating details in an organized (sequential or conceptual) manner, retaining and retrieving information, or formulating opinions.[24] Struggling to prioritize, coordinate, or delay gratification, such students find their thoughts tend to pile up as worries, leading to frustration, anxiety, and stress. Indeed, students with underdeveloped executive functions may experience the challenge as difficulties "directing mental traffic."[25]

The tragic upshot is that education, touted as the critical path out of poverty, can work for most struggling high school students only if they are provided and take advantage of extensive assistance. Their compromised executive function skills may prevent them from completing most developmentally appropriate academic tasks on their own, even if they are emotionally receptive to improving their learning.

Group 4 Passage

Example: Impaired Working Memory

Students chronically preoccupied with stressors, such as anxieties connected to poverty, tend to exhibit inordinate difficulty performing memory tasks, even under safe and otherwise favorable conditions. Stress compromises the health of the developing brain (including the critical prefrontal cortex), weakening the processing, retention, and recall of information. Furthermore, if the youth has been chronically stressed because of perceived threats to safety, the brain tends to remain preoccupied with negative or distracting thoughts, including fear of the negative consequences of failure, further hampering the executive function of working memory. Hence, even the most engaging teaching practices may not reach a student who has been chronically stressed by the threat of violence, or by other safety issues.[27]

In addition, memory encoding declines when the adrenal gland releases cortisol, a hormonal response to sustained stress. Cortisol slowly kills off cells in the hippocampus, the memory consolidation center of the brain. If high stress is chronic during development, the hippocampus is stunted, causing memory impairment, impeding the processing and recall of information. In effect, a brain regularly overloaded by stress will provide neither the capacity nor the speed a student needs to handle all the incoming information.[28]

Though the larger purpose of education is the acquisition of broad thinking skills, never simply the memorization of facts, students cannot develop effective thinking strategies without the ability to recall from their own knowledge base. Memory enables them to grow the skills to perform more complex cognitive tasks, such as comprehension, reasoning, planning, organizing, problem solving, and decision-making.

THE TAKEAWAY

In the space below, write 2-3 key points or insights you gained from reading, reflecting on, and/or discussing the main ideas in Chapter 5.

1. _____
   _____
2. _____
   _____
3. _____
   _____

Chapter 6

What Poverty Looks Like in High School: Impaired Well-Being

Learning for this chapter emphasizes how the education of students living in poverty is affected by their well-being. More specifically, students' impaired socioemotional well-being contributes to their academic underachievement and also challenges educators' efforts to achieve educational equity. The dysfunctional marriage between the school and the family, supported by the community, also contributes to this major loss, hindering youth from fulfilling their potential.

THINKING IT THROUGH

Choose one or more of the individual reflection topics below to stimulate inquiry for deepening awareness and understanding.

1. How does an adolescent's socioemotional well-being impact teacher-student and student-student relationships? Why do these relationships matter?

   _____
   _____
   _____

2. In addition to issues all adolescents usually experience, many adolescents in poverty suffer impaired socioemotional well-being due to poverty stressors. What do you think could happen if these issues are not addressed?

   _____
   _____
   _____

3. How does students' low socioemotional well-being affect educators' attempts to provide educational equity?

   _____
   _____
   _____

4. Do you believe a dysfunctional "marriage of true minds" among the school/family/community has contributed to youth's impaired socioemotional well-being? Please explain.

_____
_____
_____

EXTENSION GROUP ACTIVITY FOR FURTHER THOUGHT AND DISCUSSION

Q & A Session

Engage in a question and answer session to share opinions, insights, and understandings about Chapter 6 - "What Poverty Looks Like in High School: Impaired Well-Being."

- On the front of one index card, each participant writes a question about Chapter 6. The questions should be higher-order or open-ended, not evaluative. (This can be done before meeting time or even taking a few minutes to complete at the beginning of the meeting time.)

- Divide into groups of 3-5. Each group member asks his or her question of other group members. Reflecting on answers to each question, each member writes down interesting and unique responses or "tweetable moments" on the back of his or her index card.

- When everyone in the group has had a chance to ask a question and answer questions, group participants will come together as a whole to discuss predominant thoughts, understandings, and revelations.

- Debrief with this question: How will this information guide your teaching and learning practices?

THE TAKEAWAY

In the space below, write 2-3 key points or insights you gained from reading, reflecting on, and/or discussing the main ideas in Chapter 6.

1. _____
_____
2. _____
_____
3. _____
_____

Part II: SYNERGY TOWARD A SOLUTION

Key Points

- Schools should seek to "level the playing field" for disadvantaged high school students by providing them with a fair and equitable education through a palette of well-chosen solutions or interventions; this comprehensive approach must involve school/family/community partnerships to reengage students in learning and, more broadly, in their transitions to adulthood.

- Fairness in education is about equality and equity. While equality in education is treating every student the same, equity is giving every student the support needed to grow and be successful, removing the barriers to educational disadvantage.

- Inclusion is another aspect of equity; it is setting a basic minimum standard for education (e.g., being able to read and write) that is shared by all students regardless of background, personal characteristics, or location.

- Educational equity is a focus on what is fair and just; it means that every student—despite race, gender, ethnicity, language, disability, family backgrounds, or family income—has access to the resources and educational rigor that prepares him or her for lifelong learning, success in the workforce, and participation in representative government.

- Educational equity seeks to identify imbalances in educational advantage and performance or results for low-income and other marginalized students, and then introduces modifications intended to address or compensate for those inequities by teaching students in different ways, redesigning school programs and providing more academic support and educational services to students with the most needs.

- Equity acknowledges the different needs of individual students and how they all require specific support to be able to reach goals such as achieving proficiency on standardized tests or graduating from high school with the foundational knowledge and skills to fulfill potential and transition successfully to adult roles.

- A proactive strategy involves consciously teaching with equity as the primary goal—sometimes called social justice pedagogy or "teaching for social justice." Social justice teaching and learning practices involve truly seeing students for who they are and where they came from. Teachers recognize students as valuable contributors to classroom learning, as opposed to seeing students as academic, social, and cultural burdens.

References

The Aspen Education & Society Program and the Council of Chief State Officers (2017). *Leading for Equity: Opportunities for State Education Chiefs*. Washington, D.C.

Levitan, Joseph (2016). "The Difference Between Educational Equity, and Justice…and Why it Matters." Forum of the American Journal of Education. Retrieved from http://www.ajeforum.com/the-difference-between-educational-equality-equity-and-justice-and-why-it-matters-by-joseph-levitan/

Glossary of Education Reform. (2016). "Equity." Great Schools Partnership. Retrieved from https://www.edglossary.org/equity/

Belle, Crystal (2019). "What is Social Justice Education Anyway?" *Education Week*. Retrieved from https://www.edweek.org/ew/articles/2019/01/23/what-is-social-justice-education-anyway.html

Organisation for Economic Co-operation and Development (2008). *Ten Steps to Equity in Education*. Retrieved from http://www.oecd.org/education/school/39989494.pdf

Chapter 7

Restarting: Beyond Failed Tradition

In this chapter guide, educators will revisit public education reforms purposed to raise achievement for students in traditional or conventional high-poverty high schools serving a disproportionate number of students from low-income backgrounds. A modern-day high school program of study, on the other hand, would promote holistic education, long known as student centered learning. Educators will identify what they know and what they want to know about student-centered learning, in addition to doing some research to learn more about student-centered education.

THINKING IT THROUGH

Choose one or more of the individual reflection topics below to stimulate inquiry for deepening awareness and understanding.

1. In your opinion, which public education reforms (e.g., standards-based education) have had the most impact on the achievement of disadvantaged students?

2. To what extent is traditional public high school education part of the problem in educators' ability to provide a quality education to help all students (especially low-income youth) fulfill potential?

3. What experiences have you had with whole-child, student-centered learning approaches in the schools you have worked?

_____
_____
_____

4. The whole-child, student-centered learning practices outlined in the three case studies in this chapter show a dramatic shift from traditional teaching and learning practices. How possible is it to replicate these strategies on a large scale so that they work in all public high schools?

_____
_____
_____

EXTENSION GROUP ACTIVITY FOR FURTHER THOUGHT AND DISCUSSION
K W L Activity

A student-centered education is intended to empower and engage students. The approach is effective in closing the opportunity gap and in providing an equitable education for all students.

- Individually, complete the KWL Chart about student-centered learning on page 33. List details in the first two columns; then do an online search to finish the last column.

STUDENT-CENTERED LEARNING

K	W	L
What do I **know** about student-centered learning?	What do I **want** to know about student-centered learning?	What did I **learn** about student-centered learning?

- Next, in pairs have a conversation about the information in your chart, sharing thoughts and insights.
- Then, as a whole group, discuss the following:
  - Identify elements or examples of student-centered learning.
  - How do you make student-centered learning work for low-performing, economically disadvantaged high school students?

THE TAKEAWAY

In the space below, write 2-3 key points or insights you gained from reading, reflecting on, and/or discussing the main ideas in Chapter 7.

1. _____
2. _____
3. _____

Chapter 8

The Caring & Engaging Schools Model

Chapter 8 outlines the strengths-based, whole-child education model I call "Caring & Engaging Schools," a framework that consists of a comprehensive and integrative reform effort that will speak to the academic and socioemotional challenges many of our low-income high school students face, while benefiting all public high school youth. Teachers reflect upon their experiences, beliefs, and instructional practices, as well as examine a case study illustrating strengths-based, whole-child education practices.

THINKING IT THROUGH

Choose one or more of the individual reflection topics below to stimulate inquiry for deepening awareness and understanding.

1. What experiences have you had with deficit-based education/remediation? What were your expectations for students in terms of academic performance? How would you encourage students to use their strengths to deal with their struggles?

   _____
   _____
   _____

2. How will strengths-based, whole-child education practices build teacher-student relationships?

   _____
   _____
   _____

3. In your opinion, can a strengths-based, whole-child perspective to education help economically disadvantaged students climb out of poverty? Under what conditions?

_____
_____
_____

4. What practices in your classroom or school do you consider to be strengths-based, whole-child education approaches?

_____
_____
_____

EXTENSION GROUP ACTIVITY FOR FURTHER THOUGHT AND DISCUSSION
Case Study - Jigsaw Protocol

To create awareness about a strengths-based, whole-child approach to education, engage in a jigsaw protocol with colleagues. Everyone should read carefully the case study on pages 37-41; it is an extended version of Case Study 8.1 in Chapter 8 of *Caring & Engaging Schools*. (You may choose to read the Case Study before meeting.)

- After 10 minutes, divide into pairs, triads, groups of four, etc. to work collaboratively on the questions below. Divide the questions into equal segments, depending on the number of groups you have.

1. Why was the *My Voice* program developed? What issues or problems had to be dealt with?

_____
_____

2. How is the community involved in this endeavor?

   _____
   _____
   _____

3. What course of action did the project team take to solve the problem?

   _____
   _____
   _____

4. What type of professional learning is provided to the tutors/teachers before implementing the strengths-based, whole-child education practices? How were tutors encouraged to work on their teaching strengths?

   _____
   _____
   _____

5. Describe the engagement component of *My Voice*. How is the strengths-based philosophy incorporated into the existing curriculum?

   _____
   _____
   _____

6. Describe the well-being component of *My Voice*. How does it incorporate the whole-child philosophy and aspects of culturally responsive teaching?

   _____
   _____
   _____

7. How does the *My Voice* program engage students, promote learning, and support student development?

   _____
   _____
   _____

8. What information is provided to show that the 4-week pilot intervention was successful? Why are results significant?

   _____
   _____
   _____

- After 15-20 minutes of preparation time, each group presents its information to the whole group, displaying information on a flip chart, white board, etc.
- As a whole group, respond to these:
  - How does the *My Voice* case study impact your understanding of a strengths-based, whole-child education approach?

    _____
    _____
    _____

  - What are your teaching strengths? How do you use them to facilitate student learning?

    _____
    _____
    _____

  - Do you believe a program like this could work in your school? With adaptations?

    _____
    _____
    _____

Strengths-Based, Whole-Child Case Study: *My Voice*

In 2008 the Labor Department of New Zealand reported that a substantial number of young adults (44,000 people) aged 15-25 year-olds—mainly the Maori people—had become disengaged from the mainstream education sector, training, and employment. A disproportionate number of Maori live in poverty compared to other ethnic groups in New Zealand. The young adults had little to no formal qualifications and low literacy and numeracy skills that impeded employment or further learning opportunities. Of critical importance to New Zealand society was to reconnect this population with education. Thus, the Ako Aotearoa National Centre for Tertiary Teaching Excellence and leaders from various training and employment organizations in New Zealand formed a project team to help the targeted population return to education, either to gain employment or to progress into higher learning opportunities.

Before designing activities to help the 15-25 year-olds, the project team conducted a series of needs-analysis workshops with them, which revealed their desires to be treated like individuals, not statistics and to know what they were good at and what they could do. Four key indicators were identified as important to learners/students in the program: course engagement, hope, well-being, and tutor/teacher relationships. Learners also reported they needed help addressing a range of broader wellbeing issues such as childcare, health needs, and financial literacy.

The team then developed a student engagement program called *My Voice,* a four-week intensive pilot intervention to help youth understand their strengths, aiming to reconnect them to education, employment, and training. The program incorporated a strengths-based education philosophy and activities into the existing curriculum. It provided 59 learners with the opportunity to develop a voice or identity of their own: their own attributes, aspirations, and strengths. The strengths-based engagement framework sought to address well-being and hope, as well as relationships with tutors, focusing learners on discovering their abilities and applying their strengths to reach optimal levels of achievement rather than identifying with their weaknesses.

Recognizing the influence that educators have in engaging students in learning and creating and encouraging positive learning experiences, the tutors/teachers from the Ako Aotearoa National Centre for Tertiary Teaching Excellence went through a comprehensive training and support program. Training was designed to help tutors make a positive transition from working in a remedial environment to working in a strengths-based environment, as well as familiarizing themselves with the engagement framework prior, to delivering instruction to the targeted young adults.

Based on the assumption that students will not be engaged in learning if their tutors/teachers are not engaged in their work, the project team also developed engagement strategies to encourage tutors to work on their strengths. Training included workshops to help tutors identify the benefits and challenges of working and training in a strengths-based environment, identifying personal strengths, maximizing strengths and managing weaknesses in the workplace, and understanding how *My Voice* could be used as a strengths-based approach to enhance learner engagement, achievement, and well-being.

In the engagement component of the program, learners participated in a range of activities that helped them to understand more about themselves, their tutors, and others in the course. The intervention consisted of four phases: 1) Settling In: A Strong Start, aiming at experiencing early success with strengths-related conversations and reflections focused on questions such as "What do I like?", "What can I do?", and "What's right about me?"; 2) Discovering My Strengths, helping clarify their strengths and how they might be used to achieve goals; 3) Using My Strengths, guiding the application of strengths to engage in course activities in their own effective ways; and 4) Living My Strengths, preparing to negotiate positive transitions from classes to further study or employment aligned to their strengths.

Another part of the program included helping students rebuild their own well-being; this section of *My Voice* was based on a holistic health and well-being model of Maori principles: 1) physical ("I have the resources to do this course") – activities included those that made students feel safe, such as helping students to establish good study habits, providing effective learning resources, and supplying instruction about healthy lifestyles; 2) psychological ("I believe I can do this course") – tasks involved focusing on learners' abilities, using positive affirmations, celebrating success, understanding thoughts and feelings associated with strengths and weaknesses, and applying and using strengths to manage stress and change; 3) social ("I have the support to do this course") – activities included making connections with the tutor/teacher and other learners, creating and maintaining strong support networks, taking responsibility, and learning collaboratively; and 4) spiritual ("I can cope with the demands of this course") – relevant tasks involved providing learners with the opportunity to explore their cultural values, discover their inner strengths and own weaknesses, articulate their life and career aspirations, and set goals.

Achievement during the four-week intervention was noted by students' responses through survey data and focus groups. All participants reported positive shifts over the program duration in course engagement, hope, and well-being. Learners reported that the engagement framework provided a focus and purpose for their learning, helped them to discover and articulate strengths they did not know they had, as they also gained the ability to link strengths to future careers/jobs. The intervention made students believe they could achieve. Learner comments indicated high levels of hope for course completion and achieving future aspirations and the belief they could achieve no matter what they choose to do. Learners reported wanting to achieve, in addition to believing in themselves and what they could achieve and how they could use their strengths in their chosen careers. They also expressed increasing desires to continue further study. Additionally, students reported that positive relationships with their tutors enhanced their success in the course; they saw tutors as motivators who valued their ideas and opinions and understood how to help them learn.

Tutors also reported observations about students' progress and achievement: increased student engagement rates, increased motivation and higher aspirations, increased sense of pride, self-esteem, and self-efficacy beliefs. They noted that learners identified their strengths and saw a pathway forward to establishing the link between strengths and how they learn best, as well as the connection between knowing strengths and work opportunities. Tutors observed students who were more focused on course achievement and who understood the importance and relevance of the course content to their future aspirations. This is particularly relevant to the learners involved in the pilot study, since many of them were disengaged from the education sector and confused or disinterested in future aspirations.

References

Hay, Mike, and Campbell, Colin (2012). *Trialling and Evaluating a Strengths-Based Student Engagement Framework*. Ako Aotearoa National Centre for Tertiary Teaching Excellence. Retrieved from https://akoaotearoa.ac.nz/ download/ng/file/group-4241/trialling-and-evaluating-a-strengths-based-studentengagement-framework.pdf

"Socioeconomic Indicators." (2018). Statistics New Zealand – Ministry of Health. Retrieved from https://www.health.govt.nz/our-work/populations/maori-health/tatau-kahukura-maori-health-statistics/nga-awe-o-te-hauora-socioeconomic-determinants-health/socioeconomic-indicators

THE TAKEAWAY

In the space below, write 2-3 key points or insights you gained from reading, reflecting on, and/or discussing the main ideas in Chapter 8.

1. _____
   _____
2. _____
   _____
3. _____
   _____

Chapter 9

Interrelated Mindsets that Reengage Students: Hope

In Chapter 9's study educators will examine strategies they can intentionally use to counteract the loss of hope (discussed in Chapter 4), a mindset that hinders academic success. School leaders and teachers can improve educational equity at the school and classroom level by ensuring disadvantaged high school students have the instruction or interventions to help them regain the hope that helps them to reengage, building a foundation for lifelong success.

THINKING IT THROUGH

Choose one or more of the individual reflection topics below to stimulate inquiry for deepening awareness and understanding.

1. What is hope and why does it matter for high school students living in poverty?

2. Compare and contrast low- and high-hope students. Why is it important to know students' hope levels?

3. How can teaching students a hope mindset model—goal setting, pathways, and agency— promote and strengthen students' academic success?

4. Please describe any efforts or strategies you have used in your classroom to promote a hopeful mindset in

students. How do you think providing hope mindset instruction contributes to education equity for disadvantaged high schoolers?

_____
_____
_____

EXTENSION GROUP ACTIVITY FOR FURTHER THOUGHT AND DISCUSSION
Case Studies Discussion

Working with colleagues, review and discuss aspects of the hope mindset case studies presented in Chapter 9 of *Caring & Engaging Schools*. Transfer the case study chart on page 44 to a large piece of paper or a whiteboard; write responses in the appropriate places. Then discuss these:

- Can you use any of these strategies or interventions in your classroom/school? Why or why not?

_____
_____
_____

- Could any of the strategies work in your classroom/school if they were adapted? Explain.

_____
_____
_____

- Do you believe "Hope is the foundational antecedent to academic success" (*Caring & Engaging Schools*, p. 88)? Why or why not? What does this belief mean in terms of what we do in our classrooms/schools and how we engage the family and the community?

_____
_____
_____

Case Study Aspects	Case Study 9.1: Portuguese Middle School Students	Case Study 9.2: The Making Hope Happen High School Program
Way hope level of students is measured		
Hope-based interventions provided and length of each		
Ways interventions sought to help students		
Description of the involvement of teachers, parents, or others		
Results of study		

THE TAKEAWAY

In the space below, write 2-3 key points or insights you gained from reading, reflecting on, and/or discussing the main ideas in Chapter 9.

1. _____

2. _____

3. _____

Chapter 10

Interrelated Mindsets That Reengage Students: Growth

Many low-income students display a fixed mindset about their own possibilities and have developed the view that their talents and intelligence are static—that no possibility for improvement exists. A growth mindset, however, encourages learning and increases educators' ability to provide an equitable education. Thus, learning and development for Chapter 10 involves becoming more aware of your growth mindset beliefs and practices and creating a growth mindset plan to help disaffected low-income high school students reengage in schooling.

THINKING IT THROUGH

Choose one or more of the individual reflection topics below to stimulate inquiry for deepening awareness and understanding.

1. Have you noticed students in your classroom or school who have a fixed mindset? What characteristics do they exhibit?

   _____
   _____
   _____

2. Describe some of the strategies you have used in your classroom to help students with a fixed mindset regain their confidence. How did you promote a growth mindset?

   _____
   _____
   _____

3. How would you work with students' families or others in the community to foster a growth mindset in your students?

   _____
   _____
   _____

4. Choose one of the following quotes and explain how it illustrates the growth mindset.

   _____
   _____
   _____

- "Anyone who has never made a mistake has never tried anything new." Albert Einstein
- "Certainty is a cruel mindset. It hardens our minds against possibility." - Ellen Langer
- "Most people never run far enough on their first wind to find out they've got a second. Give your dreams all you've got and you'll be amazed at the energy that comes out of you." - William James

EXTENSION GROUP ACTIVITY FOR FURTHER THOUGHT AND DISCUSSION
Human Spectrogram Exercise: Surveying Growth Mindset Beliefs and Practices

To help you examine your growth mindset beliefs and practices, engage in a human spectrogram exercise with colleagues.
- As someone from the group reads the ten statements under "Growth Mindset Beliefs and Practices" (pages 47-48), other members of the group stand along one wall where one corner represents strongly agree and another corner represents strongly disagree. Others may choose to stand in the middle or closer to one corner, representing the degree to which they agree

or disagree. Members move in this manner as each statement is read.

- Afterwards, as a group, discuss responses and create an action plan for helping students achieve a growth mindset (include the family and community in your plan); write it in the box labeled "Growth Mindset Action Plan" (page 48).

Growth Mindset Beliefs and Practices
1. All high school students, especially those living in poverty, sorely need a growth mindset to engage in the learning that nurtures their talents and strengths.
2. All students have the potential to grow, developing their talents and strengths.
3. Growth mindset interventions help students persist and influence how they will understand and explain failures and challenges.
4. The intellectual growth and achievement of disadvantaged students is affected by not only poverty, lack of resources, impaired school/family/community relationships, and other factors but also by teacher beliefs and expectations.
5. It would help if teachers are administered growth mindset interventions; they will be enabled better to promote, teach with, and live by a mindset of growth, as well as instill the growth mindset message within their students.
6. I mostly believe that students living in poverty (even with supportive interventions) cannot use the critical thinking skills that enable them to engage in challenging tasks or achieve high academic performance.
7. Intelligence can be developed through effort, instruction, and various other means and supports.
8. I encourage my students to try harder, and I also provide them with specific feedback and learning strategies to help them improve.

9. I praise my students for their effort, persistence, and the strategies they use to obtain goals.
10. I give myself the freedom to learn, grow, and stretch to fulfill my potential.

Growth Mindset Action Plan

References

Seals, Christopher (2018). *Teacher Beliefs: Effects of a Teacher Based Mindset Intervention on Math Student Motivation and Achievement.* Dissertation

Dweck, Carol S. (2010). "Mind-sets and equitable education." *Principal Leadership*, 10(5).

THE TAKEAWAY

In the space below, write 2-3 key points or insights you gained from reading, reflecting on, and/or discussing the main ideas in Chapter 10.

1. _____
2. _____
3. _____

Chapter 11

**Interrelated Mindsets That Reengage Students:
Sense of Purpose**

Cultivating a sense of purpose mindset is necessary for reengaging under-resourced high school students in learning. Adolescents' interest in schooling stems from their belief that education is relevant to later educational, vocational, and life outcomes—that is, engaging in high school learning must be purposeful. Learning in this chapter includes determining how to help low-performing high school students succeed and fulfill their potential.

THINKING IT THROUGH

Choose one or more of the individual reflection topics below to stimulate inquiry for deepening awareness and understanding.

1. The case studies in this chapter describe sense of purpose interventions that are key to adolescent identity formation; strategies could help improve students' grades and performance, as well as spark students' interest in schoolwork that assists them in achieving self-oriented life goals and meaningful higher purpose goals. What other approaches do you think could work to help students develop a purposeful mindset?

   _____
   _____
   _____

2. In what ways have you tried to ensure that learning in your classroom is relevant to high school youth?

   _____
   _____
   _____

3. How does the power of partnership among educators, families, and the community enable high school students' expanding sense of purpose, while also promoting equity?

_____
_____
_____

4. How should hope, growth, and sense of purpose mindset instruction be integrated or addressed together in the high school curriculum so that they support and enhance each other?

_____
_____
_____

EXTENSION GROUP ACTIVITY FOR FURTHER THOUGHT AND DISCUSSION

Job Aid – Professional Development Goal and Planning Activity

In this activity you will write a goal with the intent of helping low-performing struggling high school students succeed, enabling them to fulfill potential. (*Note: Consider using a similar activity to guide and support students to set personal learning goals; goal setting promotes a sense of purpose mindset for learning and motivates students to be actively engaged in their own learning.)

- As a group, brainstorm skills or areas for improvement that will enable educator success in helping youth succeed. At the end of 10 minutes, individually choose and define your own professional development goal and write it in the "Goal Statement" box on page 51.

- Your goal statement should describe what you want to improve in or what you would like to do differently. The statement should be "SMART": specific, measurable, attainable/action-oriented, realistic, and time-based/achieved in a set time frame. The statement is not necessarily written in the order the SMART acronym is presented, but all elements should be included.

Goal Statement

- After 10 minutes, work in pairs to share goal statements and give each other feedback using the **SMART Goal Checklist** that follows. If goal statements do not meet the SMART criteria, work together to revise goals until they are well-defined.

	Yes	No
Specific		
The purpose of the goal is clear.		
It is clear what needs to be done to accomplish the goal.		
It is clear who needs to be involved or who you need to get support from to accomplish the goal.		
Measurable		
The criteria for measuring success is indicated.		
The goal statement indicates how many, or how often, or how much of something is needed to complete it.		
Attainable/Action-Oriented		
Actions to be taken that will contribute to goal attainment can be identified.		
It is possible to get the support and resources needed to accomplish the goal in the specified time frame.		
Realistic		
It is possible to achieve the stated goal by the target date.		
It is clear how the goal will help move forward the vision for achieving success.		

Time-Based		
The goal statement indicates the goal achievement date or time frame (beginning and ending dates).		
Evaluation of goal attainment to monitor progress is indicated. (optional)		

Reference

Doran, G.T. (1981) "There's a S.M.A.R.T. way to write management's goals and objectives." *Management Review* (AMA FORUM) 70 (11): 35–36.

- At the end of 10 -15 minutes, write your **Professional Development Plan** by completing the following:
    - **Action Steps** – list activities to help you reach your goal; these include practice, education or training

    _____
    _____
    _____

    - **Measurable Definition of Success** – describe how you will know when you have achieved your goal

    _____
    _____
    _____

    - **Support and Resources Needed** – identify the support and resources you need to take action on your plan

    _____
    _____
    _____

    - **Target Date** – define the schedule for starting your plan, checking progress, and meeting your goal

    _____
    _____
    _____

- After completing the plan (at the end of 15 minutes), work in pairs to share ideas and give one another feedback on the feasibility of the written plan.

THE TAKEAWAY

In the space below, write 2-3 key points or insights you gained from reading, reflecting on, and/or discussing the main ideas in Chapter 11.

1. _____
2. _____
3. _____

Chapters 12-14

Talent Development Program: Self-Regulated Learning, Tapping into Talents, and Embedded Learning

The talent development program emphasizes each student's distinct educational journey and is designed not only to help youth become college- and career-ready but also to inspire them to define their identities. Study will contribute to an understanding or awareness of practices that support youth's talent development and an examination of how the multiple intelligences approach is useful in the process of developing each student's talent.

THINKING IT THROUGH

Choose one or more of the individual reflection topics below to stimulate inquiry for deepening awareness and understanding.

1. What experiences have you had with using self-regulated learning strategies such as individual learning plans and executive functioning skills development for disadvantaged youth (or youth from higher socioeconomic levels)? How did these strategies facilitate students' talent development and improve academic achievement?

   _____
   _____
   _____

2. How does a brain-friendly strategy such as the multiple intelligences approach capitalize upon students' intellectual strengths, leading to engagement in learning?

   _____
   _____
   _____

3. What opportunities of embedded learning do you provide in your classroom or school, enabling students to grow and develop their talents?

_____
_____
_____

4. Please describe how you and/or your school enlists support from the stakeholders who comprise and augment the "marriage of true minds" partnership to develop students' talent.

_____
_____
_____

EXTENSION GROUP ACTIVITY FOR FURTHER THOUGHT AND DISCUSSION
Learning Activities Connecting with Multiple Intelligences Strengths

To gain a deeper understanding of how the multiple intelligences approach is useful in developing students' talent, plan a learning activity incorporating multiple intelligences.

- Working in pairs or triads, plan an activity that involves a combination of 3-5 multiple intelligences: verbal-linguistic, visual-spatial, interpersonal, naturalistic, logical-mathematical, intrapersonal, musical/rhythmic, and bodily-kinesthetic.
- Choose a specific academic discipline or the arts to teach a concept and give the activity a title.
- Highlight or point out the multiple intelligences being used in the activity and answer these questions:
  - How can applying the multiple intelligences approach you incorporated improve student learning?
  - What role does your multiple intelligences activity play in the development of students' talents?
- Present your group's activity to the whole group and

share/provide copies of your plan to the members of the other groups.

THE TAKEAWAY

In the space below, write 2-3 key points or insights you gained from reading, reflecting on, and/or discussing the main ideas in Chapters 12-14.

1. _____
   _____
2. _____
   _____
3. _____
   _____

Chapters 15-16

The Context of Well-Being: School-Based Mental Healthcare to Benefit All Students & Building a School-Based Mental Health Program

Study for these chapters shifts to one of the contexts in which the Caring & Engaging High School operates: student well-being, more traditionally known as mental health. Collaboration among major school stakeholders is key to the success of a holistic strengths-based perspective, which links school-based mental healthcare screenings and interventions to broader initiatives in both social and emotional learning and mindfulness training. Educators will assess the collaborative relationships at their school, as collaboration is essential for them and other school stakeholders to support more seamlessly the well-being and academic success of all high school adolescents.

THINKING IT THROUGH

Choose one or more of the individual reflection topics below to stimulate inquiry for deepening awareness and understanding.

1. In your opinion, are school-based mental health programs needed in the high school? Why or why not?

   _____
   _____
   _____

2. Why should educators pay mindful attention to students' socioemotional development?

   _____
   _____
   _____

3. How are the social and emotional learning needs of high school adolescents addressed in your school or classroom? In what areas do the socioemotional strengths of students in your classroom or school need the most development? How do the family and the community help?

_____
_____
_____

4. In your school or classroom, what experiences have you had with integrating a mental health support such as mindfulness practice? How did the practice affect student learning and behavior?

_____
_____
_____

EXTENSION GROUP ACTIVITY FOR FURTHER THOUGHT AND DISCUSSION
Inventory about Collaboration Among School Stakeholders

Developing the socioemotional or emotional intelligence strengths necessary to productively collaborate is essential for all high school stakeholders to support the well-being and academic success of all high school students.

- To assist educators in identifying the strengths and gaps in the collaborative environment at their school(s), each will individually complete the inventory on pages 59-61. It is divided into "Collaboration Among Teacher Colleagues and Between Teachers and Administrators" and "Collaboration Among the School, Family, and Community."
- In the space provided, write the number of the scale that describes collaboration at your school.
- Afterwards, choose 4-5 items from the Inventory to share your thoughts or comments with another colleague. Then have a conversation about the two questions below:

- How does your school devote time and attention to nurturing school-wide behavioral norms that undergird collaboration practices? Describe the structures, routines, and protocols used at your school to establish and facilitate teacher interactions focused on instructional and socioemotional challenges impacting learning.

_____
_____
_____

- How would collaboration among teacher colleagues and administrators advance a school improvement strategy such as a school-based mental healthcare program to benefit all students? Collaboration among the school, family, and community?

_____
_____
_____

0 Never 1 Rarely 2 Every now and then 3 Often 4 Very frequently or all the time

Collaboration Among Teacher Colleagues and Between Teachers and Administrators

_____ 1. Teachers at my school collaborate on how to best support students' academic and socioemotional needs to create and implement instructional plans linked to needs.

_____ 2. School leaders where I work invest time in establishing and maintaining a collaborative school environment, as well as set goals and expectations for meaningful collaboration.

_____ 3. My school creates the structures necessary for productive collaboration and addresses barriers that obstruct collaboration.

_____ 4. I regularly engage in routines where teachers communicate about classroom experiences to strengthen pedagogical practices in order to integrate social and emotional learning.

_____5. Teachers engage with colleagues in a discussion focused on instructional issues and hold each other accountable for achieving goals or producing work products.

_____6. Teachers at my school engage in online reflective conversations between colleagues within and across schools, including debriefing classroom challenges (academic and socioemotional), receiving feedback on practices, and identifying new pedagogical techniques to try.

_____7. Collaboration at my school is based on trust, commitment, open communication, and an appreciation for diverse ideas.

_____8. Administrators and teachers work closely together to develop and select instructional materials, assessments, learning strategies, and plan for professional development.

_____9. During various collaboration meetings or opportunities at my school, my suggestions or points of view are considered by other teachers and school administration.

_____10. I communicate and work with educational professionals in other roles, disciplines, and areas to facilitate mutual understanding and collective contributions to improve academic, social, and emotional outcomes for students.

Collaboration Among the School, Family, and Community

_____11. Strong ties exist among school personnel, parents, and the community, forming an integrated support network for students.

_____12. A high degree of "relational trust" exists among administrators, teachers, and parents.

_____13. Local community partners work with my school to support students' socioemotional development needs, and provide after-school activities, tutoring, and other school-based supports.

_____14. I communicate and connect with families in a mutually respectful, reciprocal way to set goals with families and prepare them to engage in complementing behaviors and activities that enhance student well-being.

_____15. My school partners with community organizations

to provide social and emotional learning practices to parents, complementing school-based universal interventions.

___16. The members of the collaborative school, family, and community partnership respect each other's unique contributions to student academic, social, and emotional well-being.

___17. Administrators and teachers work closely with local community groups and service providers, broadening the network of trained professionals who help students succeed.

___18. My school involves families in the decision-making process about their child's educational program, including making suggestions about academic and socioemotional interventions and providing input on program improvement matters.

___19. My school provides school-based practices to support parents in becoming partners in the effort to promote student learning, academic outcomes, and socioemotional development.

___20. My school emphasizes relationship building between families and educators that encourages working together to promote the educational experiences and school successes of students.

References

Anrig, G. (2015). "How we know collaboration works." *Educational Leadership*, 72(5).

Mourshed, M., Chijioke, C., & Barber, M. (2010). *How the world's most improved school systems keep getting better.* Washington, DC: McKinsey and Company.

Poulos, J., Culbertson, N., Piazza, P., and d'Entremont, C. (2014). *Making Space: The Value of Teacher Collaboration.* Rennie Center – Education Research and Policy. Retrieved from https://www.edvestors.org/wp-content/uploads/2016/05/EdVestors-Making-Space-The-Value-of-Teacher-Collaboration-2014.pdf

THE TAKEAWAY

In the space below, write 2-3 key points or insights you gained from reading, reflecting on, and/or discussing the main ideas in Chapters 15-16.

1. _____
_____
2. _____
_____
3. _____
_____

Chapters 17-18

The Context of Socioeconomic Integration:
School Desegregation to Benefit All Students &
Surmounting Barriers to Socioeconomic Integration

These chapters particularly address the needs of low-income high school youth while promoting change that will powerfully benefit the intellectual and socioemotional development of all students. Learning will include the following: an exploration of the challenges low-income students experience in economically segregated schools (high-poverty) and an examination of school district factors impacting economic segregation, while also evaluating integration as a tool to foster the strengths, academic achievement, and well-being of all students.

THINKING IT THROUGH

Choose one or more of the individual reflection topics below to stimulate inquiry for deepening awareness and understanding.

1. As an educator, what has been your involvement in school integration (socioeconomic and/or racial)? What integration policy was used (e.g., controlled choice)?

   _____
   _____
   _____

2. Describe some of the challenges associated with the experience. How did your school deal with the challenges? How did your school engage families and the community for support?

   _____
   _____
   _____

3. Describe any benefits you observed as a result of integration, including those for low- and higher-income students.

_____
_____
_____

4. In your opinion, what is the best way to desegregate America's public high schools (considering, of course, that desegregation begins in elementary school)? Please explain your response.

_____
_____
_____

EXTENSION GROUP ACTIVITY FOR FURTHER THOUGHT AND DISCUSSION
Affinity Diagramming Protocol

To deepen your understanding of the challenges associated with school segregation and the benefits of integration, develop an affinity diagram with colleagues.

- Divide into three equal smaller groups—1, 2, and 3—to address the problem statement and questions below:
  - Group 1 – Students in economically segregated schools (high-poverty) suffer academic, cognitive, and socioemotional challenges that impede their ability to fulfill potential and transition successfully to adult roles. (Problem Statement)
  - Group 2 – How might school district boundaries (though innocently drawn) reinforce economic segregation, keeping low-income students out, while also contributing to educational inequity?
  - Group 3 – How can socioeconomic integration of our schools foster students' strengths and holistic well-being, while eliminating barriers of inequity to academic achievement?

- Each individual brainstorms responses to the problem statement or question allotted to his or her group; for 7-10 minutes, write (5-6) ideas on post-it notes—one idea per note.
- Once brainstorming is complete, members of each group place their responses on a tabletop, whiteboard, wall, etc. (designate three different areas for each group).
- Each group then organizes its members' responses into similar categories or natural relationships, grouping or placing them side by side. Discuss why ideas fit in identified categories and how they relate to one another. If needed, move ideas around or generate more ideas. View generated ideas as your group's collective thoughts about the problem statement or question posed to your group.
- When ideas are categorized to your group's satisfaction, decide on a heading or name for each category (perhaps a maximum of 3-4 categories) to post related ideas/themes—consider using columns or squares to post information.
- Record end results on a large sheet of paper.
- Each group then presents affinity diagrams to the whole group. Include time in the presentation to address questions or comments from the other two groups.

Reference

American Society for Quality (2019). "What is an Affinity Diagram?" Retrieved from https://asq.org/quality-resources/affinity.

Graham, J. and Cleary, M. J., Eds. (2000). *Practical Tools for Continuous Improvement, Vol. 2: Problem-Solving and Planning Tools*. Miamisburg, OH: PQ Systems.

THE TAKEAWAY

In the space below, write 2-3 key points or insights you gained from reading, reflecting on, and/or discussing the main ideas in Chapters 17-18.

1. _____
_____
2. _____
_____
3. _____
_____

Chapter 19

Making Systemic Reform Happen

This chapter revisits the marriage of true minds between the school and family, supported by community members, as essential to implementing and sustaining the comprehensive reform demanded by the Caring & Engaging Schools model. Educators take a closer look at the roles involved in creating the whole-team synergy necessary to make a reality the strengths-based, whole-child education perspective of the Caring & Engaging Schools model, and ultimately the battle to achieve educational equity.

THINKING IT THROUGH

Choose one or more of the individual reflection topics below to stimulate inquiry for deepening awareness and understanding.

1. What experiences have you had with comprehensive reform initiatives seeking to achieve educational equity? How did educator professional development impact success?

2. How did your school strengthen family and community engagement in order to enhance student achievement?

3. What changes need to be made in your school for strengths-based, whole-child education practices to be implemented?

4. What do you consider to be the best way to deal with the conflicts that will inevitably arise in the effort to create synergy among the major stakeholders of the public high school, making a reality the strengths-based, whole-child perspective demanded by the Caring & Engaging Schools model?

_____
_____
_____

EXTENSION GROUP ACTIVITY FOR FURTHER THOUGHT AND DISCUSSION
Creating Synergy: Defining Roles to Build a High-Performing Team

A systemic approach to a comprehensive education reform such as strengths-based, whole-child education entails creating whole-team synergy. Synergy can be achieved if team members know their roles and responsibilities in the battle to achieve educational equity, helping students transition to adulthood and fulfill potential.

- With colleagues (groups of four), create a visual display of the roles and responsibilities of the following: principal, teacher, parents/family, and community.
- Next, share displays with the whole group.
- Afterwards, the whole group discusses these:
  - What barriers might you encounter in creating the whole-team synergy essential to making systemic reform a reality?
  - How would a "marriage of true minds" partnership address potential barriers to creating whole-team synergy?
  - How do you create harmony or cohesiveness for such a diverse team?

- As a major stakeholder in the high school ecosystem, how will your awareness of these roles change your interactions and communications with other stakeholders?

THE TAKEAWAY

In the space below, write 2-3 key points or insights you gained from reading, reflecting on, and/or discussing the main ideas in Chapter 19.

1. _____
2. _____
3. _____

Chapter 20

The Stage is Set for the Players

Professional learning for Chapter 20 reminds us that educational equity—a quality education to help all students fulfill potential—is indeed possible, if we were to intentionally instruct the whole child through strengths-based education. Educators will assess their personal beliefs about a strengths-based, whole-child approach and the practices in which they currently engage.

THINKING IT THROUGH

Choose one or more of the individual reflection topics below to stimulate inquiry for deepening awareness and understanding.

1. Review the components and contexts of the Caring & Engaging high school model. Why does the author believe that a strengths-based, whole-child approach will particularly address our struggling under-resourced students while benefiting all public high school students?

   _____
   _____
   _____

2. Do you believe a school or education built on strengths-based, whole-child education can alter the learning landscape to promote equity and social justice for economically disadvantaged high school students? Why or why not?

   _____
   _____
   _____

3. When educators resist change, they resist growth. What are some effective ways to address the needs of educators who may be resistant to a paradigm shift to a strengths-based, whole-child education perspective?

    _____
    _____
    _____

4. Nelson Mandela stated, *"Education is the most powerful weapon which you can use to change the world."* How does a strengths-based, whole-child education framework designed to achieve educational equity for all high school students (especially those living in poverty) illustrate Mandela's point?

    _____
    _____
    _____

EXTENSION GROUP ACTIVITY FOR FURTHER THOUGHT AND DISCUSSION
Strengths-Based, Whole-Child Education Beliefs and Practices

Consider the items in the chart on page 72; assess your strengths-based, whole-child education beliefs and practices.

- Individually agree or disagree with each of the 10 items, choosing the most appropriate answer in the space provided.
- After 5-7 minutes, discuss your responses in groups of four, sharing opinions and insights.
- At the end of 10 minutes, address this question as a whole group: What do the beliefs and practices mean in terms of what we do in our high schools?

How much do you agree or disagree with the following statements?	Strongly Agree	Agree	Disagree	Strongly Disagree
1. Given the proper nurturing, conditions, and resources, students can change and grow through their strengths and capacities.				
2. I believe that potential exists in all students and that educators should discover and implement learning experiences that help students realize potential.				
3. Through classroom instruction I help students make the connection among their strengths, aspirations, and goals.				
4. A strengths-based, whole-child philosophy can increase students' engagement in learning, as well as build and transform their lives.				
5. Everyone has unique strengths that can be mobilized to support healthy development and enhance well-being.				
6. I seek to enhance student strengths as opposed to deficits.				
7. I continually refine engagement and relationship-building with students in order to be more inclusive.				
8. I consider the whole-child and his or her unique capabilities when planning for instruction.				
9. I participate in professional development opportunities that enable me to develop a critical understanding of my own strengths-based practices to continually develop the necessary skills, knowledge, and approaches to achieve the best outcomes for students.				
10. Collaboration among teachers or communities of teacher learners is important for educating the whole child.				

References

Lopez, Shane J. and Louis, Michelle C. (2009). "The Principles of Strengths-Based Education." *Journal of College and Character*, 10(4).

Hammond, Wayne and Zimmerman, Rob (2012). *A Strengths-Based Perspective.* Resiliency Initiatives. Retrieved from http://shed-the-light.webs.com/documents/ RSL_STRENGTH_BASED_PERSPECTIVE.pdf

THE TAKEAWAY

In the space below, write 2-3 key points or insights you gained from reading, reflecting on, and/or discussing the main ideas in Chapter 20.

1. _____
_____
2. _____
_____
3. _____
_____

APPENDIX

PROMOTING EQUITY AND SOCIAL JUSTICE FOR ECONOMICALLY DISADVANTAGED HIGH SCHOOL STUDENTS: A STRENGTHS-BASED, WHOLE-CHILD EDUCATION APPROACH

A strengths-based, whole-child approach will enable us to disrupt the inequities of public education and provide a socially just education for economically disadvantaged high school students. The approach includes interrelated practices that address the cognitive/academic, social, emotional, and talent development of under-resourced high school students. The strategies will benefit youth from all socioeconomic backgrounds and may be implemented in individual classrooms and schoolwide, as well as integrated into existing programs and courses.

The ten interconnected practices (though not exhaustive) are essential, as they will aid youth to engage more fully in schooling, obtaining the skills they need to fulfill potential, be college (or other higher education) and career ready, and to climb out of poverty. Practices, along with descriptions of each and action steps for implementation, are outlined on pages 77-93.

STRENGTHS-BASED, WHOLE-CHILD EDUCATION

1. Teach with strengths (strengths-based teaching)

Description of Practice	Action Steps for Implementation
☐ Teaching effectiveness is shaped by an educator's talents/strengths (e.g., creativity, open-mindedness)—what he/she does well. Talents/strengths are the kinds of instructional activities or tasks the educator keeps coming back to time and time again, regardless of the strategies he/she had originally planned.	√ Become aware of teaching talents/strengths by completing an online assessment, making a list of activities or tasks that most energize and engage you, and/or invite another teacher to observe and give you feedback about strengths manifested during the observation.
☐ An educator's greatest opportunity for improvement, however, lies in using and developing strengths—not in trying to make up for weaknesses but in applying strengths to manage weaknesses.	√ Seek to understand and develop talents/strengths through knowledge, skills, and learning. Engage in continuous strengths-based reflective practice to develop a critical understanding of your values and professional practices and how they impact student learning and development.
☐ Despite natural teaching strengths, educators adjust teaching style to support diverse learners in order to be effective.	√ Leverage own strengths; however, include other instructional practices and skills outside of natural strengths to support student learning and talent development (e.g., You may thrive when teaching in a quiet classroom but may need to adjust when having classroom discussions).

2. Incorporate culturally responsive teaching practices

Description of Practice	Action Steps for Implementation
☐ Culturally responsive teaching is a pedagogical approach that requires educators to deeply learn about the diverse backgrounds of the students they teach.	√ Assess own behavior to uncover and disabuse self of biases; unlearn prejudices and miseducation that may be affecting the potential baggage you bring into the classroom about other cultures. Take the time to learn about and understand the things that affect student learning, including demographics and student strengths, concerns, conflicts, and challenges.
☐ Teachers appreciate and nurture distinct ethnic and other cultural strengths across all academic disciplines to encourage academic achievement and socioemotional well-being.	√ Make the classroom a judge free zone where students are empowered to look at various situations about culture with an unbiased opinion and feel comfortable asking questions to further their understanding. This may involve collaborating with colleagues, administrators, educational professionals, and parents/families to ensure success.
☐ Educators engage students and create social justice classrooms by acknowledging and valuing what students bring to the classroom.	√ Create a safe, inclusive, respectful, and equitable learning environment for all students by including all cultures in instructional practices. Enrich the curriculum by connecting to and honoring students' cultures, backgrounds, and experiences (e.g., include use of personal narratives or incorporate identity-based responses into academic study).

3. Assess students' cognitive/intellectual and socioemotional strengths

Description of Practice	Action Steps for Implementation
☐ Assessing cognitive or intellectual strengths—skills or abilities used in the processing of information necessary for engaging in learning or accomplishing all sorts of tasks—is a way to measure cognitive capacity.	√ Use executive functioning assessments (e.g., observations, interviews, various executive functioning tests) to measure students' cognitive abilities, including being able to pay attention, shift from one task or situation to another, plan, sequence, and organize information for problem solving; and use cognitive processes such as working memory and inhibitory control. Make use of various online multiple intelligences (MI) inventories to make students aware of the unique set of cognitive strengths they possess and to assess the different ways they are intelligent: verbal-linguistic, visual-spatial, interpersonal, naturalistic, logical-mathematical, intrapersonal, musical/rhythmic, and bodily-kinesthetic.
☐ Assessing socioemotional strengths is a means to inform practice, with an intentional focus on understanding students' development of social and emotional competencies and improving social and emotional learning-related instruction and programing.	√ Use socioemotional assessments (e.g., observations, interviews, self-reports, universal and targeted screening and progress monitoring) to measure students' ability to manage and express emotions, make and sustain positive relationships, and communicate ideas and feelings.

4. Develop students' cognitive/intellectual and socioemotional strengths

Description of Practice	Action Steps for Implementation
☐ Building cognitive/intellectual strengths are important to developing students' talent. Developing these strengths are considerably more critical to students' economic outcomes than are traditional measures of academic success such as course grades or test scores. These abilities are clearly predictive of job performance and other measures of life satisfaction. Expanding executive functioning skills and using the MI method build cognitive or intellectual strengths: ■ Executive functioning skills - requisite for focusing on learning, workforce success, maintaining close relationships, raising children, and generally getting along with others in the world	√ Develop executive functioning skills by: • cultivating students' self-regulation skills to enable management of academic learning and positive behavior; • defining specific executive functions, referring to them clearly and frequently as tools to help students manage their own learning; • providing opportunities for students to put their executive functions to work (e.g., articulating learning goals); • stating explicitly the purpose for a learning activity and demonstrating the steps involved: (e.g., planning, implementing); and • using strategies that support working memory.

4. Develop students' cognitive/intellectual and socioemotional strengths (cont'd)

Description of Practice	Action Steps for Implementation
■ The MI approach – 1) inspires methods for reaching all students, enabling educators to foster in students the levels and types of engagement that contribute to academic performance—even, including over time, achievement on high stakes tests and standards-based assessments; and 2) enables adolescents to better understand how their minds learn and allows them to draw upon MI strengths to demonstrate learning, helping them to make informed academic and career moves	√ Employ the MI framework by: • diagnosing how best to develop each student, based upon MI strengths and inclinations; • instructing students on how to draw on several of their strengths to experience high academic performance; • offering multiple entry points to content, providing a reasonable variety of intelligence-based options (whichever are most relevant or effective for each concept); offer multiple forms of assessment to evaluate achievement; and • creating interdisciplinary curricula, requiring students to practice and apply the diverse skills they have cultivated across topics and learning approaches.

4. Develop students' cognitive/intellectual and socioemotional strengths (cont'd)

Description of Practice	Action Steps for Implementation
☐ Building students' socioemotional or inner strengths is also an important part of developing their talent. Socioemotional skills help ensure students are prepared for the world of work; they are just as reliable a predictor of career-readiness as cognitive skills.	√ Develop socioemotional strengths by: • providing social and emotional learning—direct instruction on how to understand and manage emotions, set and achieve positive goals, feel and show empathy for others, establish and maintain positive relationships, make responsible decisions, and develop the socio-emotional capacity to balance the internal and external worlds; • integrating socioemotional instruction with academic content, and general teaching practices that support students' social and emotional competency growth; and • acknowledging and reacting to students' teamwork, interactions, motivation, engagement, emotional states, relationships, self-awareness, self-regulation and many other characteristics, behaviors, and dispositions.

5. Offer goal setting instruction

Description of Practice	Action Steps for Implementation
☐ Goal setting instruction involves helping students develop an action plan or road map to motivate and guide them in tackling goals set for academic learning and beyond. ☐ Assisting students with setting personal and socioemotional learning goals is a way to prepare them for postsecondary education, the workforce, and life. 1) Personal learning goals are the ones a student identifies as important to his own learning and may be related to school subjects (e.g., improving math grades), work habit behaviors (e.g., dedicating more time to studying), learning domains (e.g., acquiring knowledge and skills), or a combination of these. 2) Socioemotional goals are those a student identifies as essential to preparing her to participate in her school and community as an intact, socially responsible individual. Goals are based on developing competencies in these areas: self-awareness, self-management, social awareness, relationship skills, and responsible decision-making. ☐ Teaching students to pursue goals enables them to think realistically about their future fulfillment of dreams and personal potential and engagement in their own unfolding.	√ Help students learn how to set and write SMART personal and socioemotional learning goals that are specific, measurable, attainable, results-focused, and achieved in a set timeframe. Goals are challenging and related to their talents, skills, and strengths. Co-create SMART goals with students, especially if they have not set goals for themselves before. This may involve helping students create a personalized or individual learning plan to pull together goals, strengths, and needs. Have students read written goals often to remind and motivate themselves about what they hope to accomplish. √ Teach students how to devise plans to achieve goals, how to experiment with strategies and methods for pursuing goals, and how to use their identified strengths as vehicles for monitoring and evaluating goal progress.

6. Provide mindset instruction

Description of Practice	Action Steps for Implementation
☐ Mindsets are core assumptions or beliefs that guide thinking and attitudes and powerfully determine interpretations of and responses to situations. Drivers of academic perseverance and academic behaviors necessary for deeper learning outcomes, constructive mindsets boost student agency, promote resilience, and promote academic self-efficacy (a student's perception that he can achieve academic success). ☐ Constructive mindsets have everything to do with a student's overall ability to function properly, both emotionally and behaviorally—in in- and out-of-school contexts. Building positive mindsets is foundational to preparing students to be lifelong learners and for using their minds to plan for the future and strategize to pursue goals. ☐ Instruction on interrelated constructive mindsets such as hope, growth, and sense of purpose is designed to strengthen and empower students to transform into a mode of high academic performance and career expectation.	

6. Provide mindset instruction (cont'd)

Description of Practice	Action Steps for Implementation
■ Hope - faith that the future can be better but is sustained by the belief that success will come as a result of the actions one takes to improve ■ Growth - the belief that intelligence is not fixed and the conviction that one's intelligence has the potential to change and grow, in ways that may not even be foreseeable, through learning	√ Offer **hope mindset instruction.** Build students hope levels and hopeful thinking to get them to buy into their futures. Teach students a hope model that consists of: 1) writing goals – write down desires or aims (what they are hoping for or wish to achieve through academic learning). (See practice #5); 2) identifying pathways – list several routes or strategies to achieve goals; and 3) initiating agency – name the actions to sustain the application of those strategies (acting on pathways to facilitate an "I can do this" attitude). √ Provide **growth mindset instruction.** Teach students that their talents and abilities are not fixed but can grow or be further developed through effort, practice, instruction, and persistence. This involves: 1) including information about the brain as a muscle that can be strengthened through learning and encouraging students with growth mindset messages (e.g., "Your brain grows new connections every time you practice. It becomes smarter with hard work."); 2) teaching students to believe in their abilities to embrace the challenges and complexities of learning, also explaining the importance of positive self-talk and how it can lead to positive outcomes; and 3) inspiring students to do more by teaching them that effort is positive and by showing them the value and purpose of persistence.

6. Provide mindset instruction (cont'd)

Description of Practice	Action Steps for Implementation
■ *Sense of purpose* - the motivation that stimulates effort to progress toward learning goals and a satisfying future, helping students to relate schoolwork to paths in becoming their future selves, as well as to broader impacts that they may not fully envision yet	√ Provide **sense of purpose mindset interventions.** Instruct youth on how setting goals, classroom learning, and other activities can help guide them to finding a sense of purpose. This includes imparting: 1) instruction on self-oriented goals-goals students set that assist them with aspirations for obtaining enjoyable work matched to their talents and interests and/or for financial sustainability. Explain to students how classroom learning is relevant to these objectives and have them read stories about how doing well in school can help them achieve goals; and 2) instruction on beyond-the-self goals — goals students set because they are motivated by a higher purpose and want a meaningful and significant life. Explain to students how service learning and community service are ways to contribute to the community that will help them achieve these goals; have students write about ways they wished the world were a better place, also identifying strategies for making a positive impact on society.

7. Implement mixed ability instruction

Description of Practice	Action Steps for Implementation
☐ A mixed ability classroom is designed to promote greater equity among students, who may have otherwise been tracked and grouped along racial and socioeconomic lines, creating disparities between students and exacerbating achievement gaps. ☐ In mixed proficiency classrooms, lower-performing students are motivated to take advantage of opportunities to enhance their own preparation for college or other postsecondary training. Heterogeneous learning and grouping could establish the necessary conditions for increasing motivation, engagement, collaboration, and academic performance.	√ Intermingle students of all levels, while educating in a manner that ensures lower-achieving students are supported while the academic progress of higher-achievers goes unimpeded; use scaffolding to support students of different proficiency levels. Use complex instruction, a strategy designed to ensure equal access to learning opportunities for all students, recognizing that proficiency need not indicate fixed ability. The approach has three components: 1) multiple-ability curricula that provide varied tasks all contributing to a group effort; 2) instructional techniques that produce defined roles and cooperative social norms for group work; and 3) explicit strategies to address status problems—bringing students who are socially isolated or appear to lack academic skills into full participation, by broadening classroom perceptions of intelligence.

7. Implement mixed ability instruction (cont'd)

Description of Practice

☐ Mixed-ability instruction gives students of various backgrounds and abilities access to the same high-quality instruction and resources. Struggling students benefit from the modeling of their higher-achieving peers, while higher-achieving students are challenged to articulate their understanding for their classmates. All students are held to high standards and are encouraged to use each other as resources. Meanwhile educators unlock learning opportunities for students and are enabled to emphasize and capitalize upon the strengths of each student.

Action Steps for Implementation

√ Differentiate instruction based on students' demonstrated strengths, needs, and areas for growth; this includes offering answer and essay items, independent projects, portfolios). Employ jigsaw teaching, a differentiated and cooperative learning instructional strategy that brings together low-performing and higher-performing students to create "balanced" or equitable teams. Students work collaboratively, interact, and share knowledge and information, working on a different aspect or "piece of the puzzle" of the assigned activity.

8. Give feedback

Description of Practice	Action Steps for Implementation
☐ Feedback consists of explanations to students that provide them with insight on how to improve performance or correct mistakes; it encourages further study. ☐ Feedback assists students with understanding their process of learning (metacognition) and helps them become self-regulated learners who are aware of their most effective strategies for learning, appropriately applying and using strategies to enhance their learning and improve academic performance. ☐ Effective feedback requires that a student has a goal, takes action to achieve the goal, and receives goal-related information about his actions; feedback is information about how a student is doing in his efforts to reach a learning goal.	√ Involve students in the process of collecting and analyzing performance-based data about their learning; this helps them develop an awareness of their learning, recognize their mistakes more easily, and eventually develop strategies for tackling weak points using their strengths. √ Provide helpful feedback to students that references goals; is tangible and transparent; is connected to actions; is specific, understandable, and personalized; and is timely, ongoing, and consistent. Acknowledge the actions, choices, and responses that lead to goal attainment. Give feedback about how students process tasks, self-regulate learning, and use their ability to manage emotions and behavior to complete tasks and achieve learning goals. Talk about goals within the context of students' personal strengths, giving feedback to affirm strengths in order to build confidence, as well as provide corrective feedback to students to call attention to talents/strengths that can be further developed and used to achieve goals.

9. Offer learning support opportunities

Description of Practice	Action Steps for Implementation
☐ Learning support opportunities can improve each student's learning and development and motivation. ☐ Learning support opportunities should help students become self-regulated learners. ☐ Learning supports help students feel school connectedness—the trust that teachers/adults in the school care about their learning and about them as individuals.	√ Teach students how to self-regulate learning; this includes showing them how to set learning goals and analyze academic tasks, how to select among learning strategies, and how to self-assess performance—in particular, how to evaluate their own effectiveness using chosen cognitive strategies. √ Provide one-on-one meetings as a way to help high- and low-achieving students individually, building students' confidence and showing you are interested in helping them understand course content and in improving. Deliver study skills interventions to improve learning, facilitating students' success in high school and preparation for higher education and the workforce. Consider using peer tutors in the classroom or assigning students as study partners based on complementing strengths.

9. Offer learning support opportunities (cont'd)

Description of Practice	Action Steps for Implementation
☐ Supports enable students to be successful in high school and be prepared to take advantage of the range of opportunities that await them after high school.	√ Refer students to school-based mentoring opportunities (if available). Mentors can provide support such as advice or insights that help students engage/reengage in school, apply to college or higher education, or find a job; mentors can also offer tangible resources or actions such as introducing a potential employer and facilitating a college visit.

10. Engage families and communities

Description of Practice	Action Steps for Implementation
☐ A strengths-based, whole-child approach to promote equity and socially just education for economically disadvantaged high school students (and students of all socioeconomic backgrounds) cannot be accomplished in isolation but in collaboration. 1)The approach is viewed as a process of empowerment, in which educators engage with families and the community—all contribute to students' learning and success. 2) The collaboration involves fostering alliances among the school, families, and the community; forming common goals, and sharing information and resources. 3)The collaboration is an invitation to be facilitators of change, with a reminder that a fair and quality education to help youth realize full potential is indeed possible.	√ Co-construct educational collaboration strategies with students and families, including collaborative assessment and goal setting for students. Facilitate parent participation in helping students figure out who they are and what strengths they have; work with parents to show them how to help students develop those strengths. Openly address obstacles, including social disadvantage and cultural differences, providing meaningful opportunities for all families to engage. Provide ongoing and open two-way communication through everyday conversations, parent-teacher conferences, written notes, emails, home visits, and participation in program or extracurricular activities. Engage the community (includes not only residents—with or without children—near students' homes and schools, but also all businesses and organizations—whether physical or virtual—that influence learning and development). The community can provide perspectives, knowledge, and other resources to support educators; this also includes working with the community to provide parent education or workshops.

10. Engage families and communities (cont'd)

Description of Practice	Action Steps for Implementation
	Enlist support from the community in providing diverse embedded learning opportunities, nourishing students' talents and developing strengths in relevant, meaningful real-world settings that enable authentic career exploration. Support includes supplying resources such as work-based learning, service learning, community service opportunities, tutoring, mentoring, and financial literacy workshops.

APPENDIX REFERENCES

Teach with strengths (strengths-based teaching)

Anderson, Edward (2004). *What is Strengths-Based Education? A Tentative Answer by Someone Who Strives to Be a Strengths-Based Educator.* Retrieved from http://strengths.uark.edu/documents/what-is-strengths-based-education.pdf

Cleaver, Samantha (2013). "How to Identify and Maximize Your Unique Talents and Strengths Educator." We Are Teachers. Retrieved from https://www.weareteachers.com/teach-to-your-strengths/

Finlay, Linda (2008). *Reflecting on 'Reflective Practice.'* PBPL52. Retrieved from https://www.open.ac.uk/opencetl/sites/www.open.ac.uk.opencetl/files/files/ecms/web-content/Finlay-(2008)-Reflecting-on-reflective-practice-PBPL-paper-52.pdf

Garmon, M. Arthur. (2004). "Changing Preservice Teachers' Attitudes/Beliefs About Diversity." *Journal of Teacher Education*, 55(3).

Hammond, Wayne and Zimmerman, Rob (2012). *A Strengths-Based Perspective.* Retrieved from https://shed-the-light.webs.com/documents/RSL_STRENGTH_BASED_PERSPECTIVE.pdf

Lane, Sheila, Lacefield-Parchini, N., and Isek, J. (2003). "Developing Novice Teachers as Change Agents: Student Teacher Placements 'Against the Grain.'" *Teacher Education Quarterly*, 55-68.

Lopez, Shane J. and Louis, Michelle C. (2009). "The Principles of Strengths-Based Education." *Journal of College and Character*, 10(4).

Resiliency Initiatives. (2011). *Embracing a Strength-Based Perspective and Practice in Education.* Retrieved from http://www.ayscbc.org/Strengths-Based%20School%20Culture%20and%20Practice.pdf

Incorporate culturally responsive teaching practices

Deady, Kathy (2017). "5 Steps to Becoming a Culturally Responsive Teacher." Retrieved from https://www.teachaway.com/blog/5-steps-becoming-culturally-responsive-teacher

Dell' Angelo, Tabitha (2014). "Creating Classrooms for Social Justice." Retrieved from https://www.edutopia.org/blog/creating-classrooms-for-social-justice-tabitha-dellangelo

Kozleski, Elizabeth B. (2000). *Culturally Responsive Teaching Matters!* Equity Alliance. Retrieved from http://guide.swiftschools.org/sites/default/files/documents/CulturallyResponsiveTeaching-Matters.pdf

Krasnoff, Basha (2016). *Culturally Responsive Teaching: A Guide to Evidence-Based Practices for Teaching All Students Equitably.* Retrieved from https://educationnorthwest.org/sites/default/files/resources/culturally-responsive-teaching.pdf

Lynch, Matthew (2012). *"What Is Culturally Responsive Pedagogy?"* Huffington Post. Retrieved from http://www.huffingtonpost.com/matthew-lynch-edd/culturally-responsivepedagogy_b_1147364.html

Assess students' cognitive/intellectual and socioemotional strengths

Center on Brain Research Injury and Training. (2010). "School-Based Assessment of Executive Function." Retrieved from https://www.brainline.org/article/school-based-assessment-executive-functions

Denham, Susanne (2016). "Tools to Assess Social and Emotional Learning in Schools." Retrieved from https://www.edutopia.org/blog/tools-assess-sel-in-schools-susanne-a-denham

Deno, S. L., Reschly, A. L., Lembke, E. S., Magnusson, D., Callender, S. A., Windram, H., and Stachel, N. (2009). "Developing a school-wide progress-monitoring system." *Psychology in the Schools*, 46, 44-55. doi: 10.1002/pits

Durlak, J. A., Weissberg, R. P., Dymnicki, A. B., Taylor, R. D., and Schellinger, K. B. (2011). "The impact of enhancing students' social and emotional learning: A meta-analysis of school-based universal interventions." *Child Development*, 82(1).

Epstein, M. H., Hertzog, M. A., and Reid, R. (2001). "The Behavioral and emotional rating scale: Long term test–retest reliability." *Behavioral Disorders*, 26(4).

Evans, Gary W. and Kim, Pilyoung (2013). "Childhood poverty, chronic stress, self-regulation, and coping." *Child Development Perspectives*, 7(1).

Gardner, Howard (1991). *The Unschooled Mind: How Children Think and How Schools Should Teach*. New York: Basic Books.

Hammond, Wayne & Zimmerman Rob. *A Strengths-Based Perspective*. Retrieved from https://www.esd.ca/Programs/Resiliency/Documents/RSL_STRENGTH_BASED_PERSPECTIVE.pdf

Kelly, Kate. "Types of Tests for Executive Functioning Issues." Retrieved from https://www.understood.org/en/school-learning/evaluations/types-of-tests/tests-for-executive-functioning-issues#

Klinger, D.A., McDivitt, P.R., Howard, B.B., Munoz, M.A., Rogers, W.T., & Wylie, E.C. (2015). *The Classroom Assessment Standards for PreK-12 Teachers*. Kindle Direct Press.

Le, Cecilia and Wolfe, Rebecca E. (2013). "How can schools boost students' self-regulation?" *Phi Delta Kappan*, 95(2).

Lopez, Shane J. and Louis, Michelle C. (2009). "The Principles of Strengths-Based Education." *Journal of College and Character*, 10(4).

McDevitt, Teresa M. and Ormrod, Jeanne Ellis (2010). *Child Development and Education, 4th Edition*. New Jersey: Pearson Education.

Nickerson, Amanda B. and Fishman Callen E. (2013). "Promoting mental health and resilience through strength-based assessment in US schools." *Educational & Child Psychology*, (30)4.

Pianta, R. C., Hamre, B. K., and Allen, J.P. (2012). "Teacher-student relationships and engagement: Conceptualizing, measuring, and improving the capacity of classroom interactions." In S. Christenson, A. Reschly, and C. Wylie (Eds.), *Handbook of Research on Student Engagement*. Boston, MA: Springer

Thapa, A., Cohen, J., Guffey, S., & Higgins-D'Alessandro, A. (2013). "A review of school climate research." *Review of educational research*, 83(3).

Develop students' cognitive/intellectual and socioemotional strengths

Armstrong, Thomas (2009). *Multiple Intelligences in the Classroom, 3rd Edition*. Alexandria, Va.: ASCD.

Babcock, Elisabeth D. (2014). *Using Brain Science to Design New Pathways Out of Poverty*. Crittenton Women's Union. Retrieved from https://s3.amazonaws.com/empath-website/pdf/Research-UsingBrainScienceDesignPathwaysPover ty-0114.pdf

Bailey, Francis and Pransky, Ken (2014). *Memory at Work in the Classroom: Strategies to Help Underachieving Students*. Alexandria, Va.: ASCD.

Bromley, E., Johnson, J. G., and Cohen, P. (2006). "Personality strengths in adolescence and decreased risk of developing mental health problems in early adulthood." *Comprehensive Psychiatry*, 47(4).

Burke, Christine A. (2010). "Mindfulness-based approaches with children and adolescents: A Preliminary review of current research in an emergent field." *Journal of Child and Family Studies*, 19(2).

Collaborative for Academic, Social, and Emotional Learning (CASEL). "Core SEL Competencies." Retrieved from https://casel.org/core-competencies/

Center on the Developing Child, Harvard University (2011). *Building the Brain's "Air Traffic Control" System: How Early Experiences Shape the Development of Executive Function (Working Paper No. 11)*. Retrieved from http://www.developingchild.harvard.edu

Center on the Developing Child, Harvard University (2015). *Enhancing and Practicing Executive Function Skills with Children from Infancy to Adolescence*. Retrieved from http://www.developingchild.harvard.edu

Chaban, Peter and Tannock, Rosemary (2009). "ADHD and Executive Function." AboutKidsHealth. Retrieved from http://www.aboutkidshealth.ca/En/ResourceCentres/ADHD/AboutADHD/ADHDandBrainFunction/Pages/ADHDand-Executive-Function.aspx

Clonan, S. M., Chafouleas, S. M., McDougal, J. L., and Riley-Tillman, T. C. (2004). "Positive psychology goes to school: Are we there yet?" *Psychology in the Schools*, 41(1).

Darling-Hammond, L., Austin, K., Lit, I., Martin, D., and Gardner, H. (2003). "Different kinds of smart: Multiple intelligences." *Session 4 of The Learning Classroom: Theory Into Practice*. Annenberg Learner. Retrieved from https:// www.learner.org/courses/learningclassroom/support/04_mult_intel.pdf

Edutopia (2009). *Big Thinkers: Howard Gardner on Multiple Intelligences*. Retrieved from https://www.edutopia.org/multiple-intelligences-howard-gardner video.

Elias, Maurice J. (2004). "Academic and social-emotional learning." *Educational Practices Series*, International Academy of Education. Retrieved from https://www.unicef.org/eapro/3A_Academic_SEL.pdf

Gable, Shelly L. and Haidt, Jonathan (2005). "What (and why) is positive psychology?" *Review of General Psychology*, 9(2)

Goldstein, S., Naglieri, J. A., Princiotta, D., and Otero, T. M. (2014). "Introduction: A History of executive functioning as a theoretical and clinical construct." In S. Goldstein and J. A. Naglieri (Eds.), *Handbook of Executive Functioning*. New York: Springer. Retrieved from https://www.dvfs.org/uploaded/ library/LDIQ_Resources/LDIQ_Photos/Chap_1_Goldstein_Handbook_of_ EF_81012.pdf

Jimerson, S. R., Sharkey, J. D., Nyborg, V. and Furlong, Michael J. (2004). "Strength-based assessment and school psychology: A Summary and synthesis." *The California School Psychologist*, 9(1).

Kabat-Zinn, Jon (2003). "Mindfulness-based interventions in context: Past, present, and future." *Clinical Psychology: Science and Practice*, 10(2).

Klingberg, Torkel (2010). "Training and plasticity of working memory." *Trends in Cognitive Sciences*, 14(7).

Krasnoff, Basha (2016). *Culturally Responsive Teaching: A Guide to Evidence-Based Practices for Teaching All Students Equitably*. Retrieved from https://educationnorthwest.org/sites/default/files/resources/culturally-responsive-teaching.pdf

Lawson, G. M., Hook, C. J., Hackman, D. A., and Farah, M. J. (2015). "Socioeconomic status and neurocognitive development: executive functions." In J. A. Griffin, P. McCardle, and L. Freund (Eds.), *Executive Function in Preschool-Age Children: Integrating Measurement, Neurodevelopment, and Translational Research*. Washington, D.C.: American Psychological Association Press.

Mattern, K., Burrus, J., Camara, W., O'Connor, R., Hansen, M. A., Gambrell, J., Casillas, A., and Bobek, B. (2014). *Broadening the Definition of College and Career Readiness: A Holistic Approach*. ACT Research Report Series. Retrieved from http://files.eric.ed.gov/fulltext/ED555591.pdf

Melter, Lynn (Ed.) (2007). *Executive Function in Education: From Theory to Practice*. New York: The Guilford Press.

Morrison, William and Kirby, Patricia (2010). *Schools as a Setting for Promoting Positive Mental Health: Better Practices and Perspectives. Joint Consortium for School Health, Canada.* Retrieved from http://www.jcsh-cces.ca/ upload/JCSH%20Positive%20 Mental%20Health%20Perspectives%20Better%20 Practices.PDF

National Association of School Psychologists (2015). *Supporting Students' Resilience in the School and Community.* Retrieved from https://www.nasponline. org/Documents/Research%20and%20Policy/Research%20Center/Supporting_Resilience_Research.pdf

Pellegrino, James W. and Hilton, Margaret L. (Eds.) (2012). *Education for Life and Work Developing Transferable Knowledge and Skills in the 21st Century.* National Research Council. Retrieved from https://www.nap.edu/catalog/13398/ education-for-life-and-work-developing-transferable-knowledge-and-skills

Pianta R.C., Hamre B.K., Allen J.P. (2012) "Teacher-Student Relationships and Engagement: Conceptualizing, Measuring, and Improving the Capacity of Classroom Interactions." In S. Christenson, A. Reschly, and C. Wylie (Eds.), *Handbook of Research on Student Engagement.* Boston, MA: Springer

Resiliency Initiatives. (2011). *Embracing a Strength-Based Perspective and Practice in Education.* Retrieved from http://www.ayscbc.org/Strengths-Based%20School%20 Culture%20and%20Practice.pdf

Sparks, Sarah D. (2019). "Why Teacher-Student Relationships Matter." *Education Week,* 38(25).

Willis, Judy (2011). "Whose Children Will Get the Best Jobs in the 21st Century?" Psychology Today. Retrieved from https://www.psychologytoday.com/ blog/radical-teaching/201104/whose-children-will-get-the-best-jobs-in-the-21stcentury

Wilson, Donna (2015). "Strategies for Strengthening the Brain's Executive Functions." Edutopia: George Lucas Education Foundation. Retrieved from http:// www.edutopia.org/blog/strategies-strengthening-brains-executive-functionsdonna-wilson-marcus-conyers

Yoder, Nicholas (2014). *Teaching the Whole Child: Instructional Practices That Support Social-Emotional Learning in Three Teacher Evaluation Frameworks, Revised Edition.* Retrieved from https://gtlcenter.org/sites/default/files/TeachingtheWholeChild.pdf

Zenner, C., Herrnleben-Kurz, S., and Walac, H. (2014). "Mindfulness-based interventions in schools—a systematic review and meta-analysis." *Frontiers in Psychology,* 5.

Offer goal setting instruction

Covington, Martin V. (2000). "Goal theory, motivation, and school achievement: An Integrative review." *Annual Review of Psychology,* 5.

Dweck, Carol S. (1986). "Motivational processes affecting learning." *American Psychologist,* 41(10).

Lee, Saeyun D. (2019) *Success Plans: Promising Tools for Customizing Student Supports and Opportunities.* Cambridge, MA: Education Redesign Lab.

Lopez, S. J., Rose, S., Robinson, C., Marques, S. C., and Pais-Ribeiro, J. (2014). "Measuring and promoting hope in schoolchildren." In M. J. Furlong, R. Gilman, and E. S. Huebner (Eds.), *Handbook of Positive Psychology in Schools, 2nd Edition.* New York: Taylor & Francis.

National Association for College Admission Counseling (2015). *Individual Learning Plans for College and Career Readiness: State Policies and School-Based Practices (A National Study).* Hobsons. Retrieved from https://www. nacacnet.org/globalassets/documents/publications/research/nacacilpreport.pdf

Willis, Judy (2011). "Whose children will get the best jobs in the 21st century?" Psychology Today. Retrieved from https://www.psychologytoday.com/blog/ radical-teaching/201104/whose-children-will-get-the-best-jobs-in-the-21stcentury

Wolters, Christopher A. (2010). *Self-Regulated Learning and the 21st Century Competencies*. Retrieved fromhttps://pdfs.semanticscholar.org/6765/d44879f6dceba363c-7cf9db19e88e12bde4e.pdf

Solberg, V. Scott, Martin, Judith, Larson, Mindy, Nichols, Kathryn, Booth, Heidi, Lillis, Jennifer, and Costa, Lee. (2018). *Promoting Quality Individualized Learning Plans Throughout the Lifespan: A Revised and Updated "ILP HOW TO GUIDE 2.0."* Retrieved from https://careertech.org/resource/promoting-quality-individualized-learning-plans-throughout-lifespan-revised-updated-ilp-guide

Provide mindset instruction

Anderson, E. C. (2000, February). *Affirming students' strengths in the critical years.* Paper presented at the National Conference on the First Year Experience, Columbia, SC.

Aronson, J. (2004). "The threat of stereotype." *Educational Leadership*, 62(3).

Busteed, Brandon H. (2014). "Make a Difference: Show Students You Care." *Education Week*, 34(6).

Blackwell, L. S., Trzesniewski, K. H., and Dweck, C. S. (2007). "Implicit theories of intelligence predict achievement across an adolescent transition: A Longitudinal study and an intervention." *Child Development*, 78(1).

Claro, S., Paunesku, D., and Dweck, C. S. (2016). *Growth Mindset Tempers the Effects of Poverty on Academic Achievement. Proceedings of the National Academy of Sciences.* Retrieved from https://web.stanford.edu/~paunesku/articles/ claro_2016.pdf Claro, Susana and Paunesku, David (2014). Mindset Gap among SES Groups: The Case of Chile with Census Data. Presented at Society for Research on Educational Effectiveness conference. Retrieved from https://www.sree.org/ conferences/2014f/program/downloads/abstracts/1304.pdf

Dell' Angelo, Tabitha (2014). "Creating Classrooms for Social Justice." Retrieved from https://www.edutopia.org/blog/creating-classrooms-for-social-justice-tabitha-dellangelo

Dunman, Elisa, Hall, Karen, Hulme, Eileen, and Klinger, Karin. "Best Practices for Developing a Strengths Approach to Student Development." Retrieved from https://www.weber.edu/WSUImages/leadership/docs/sq/azusa/leadership/best-practices-strengths-approach-student-dev.pdf

Dweck, Carol S. (2006). *Mindset: The New Psychology of Success.* New York: Ballantine Books.

Dweck, Carol S. (2008). "Brainology: Transforming students' motivation to learn." *Independent School Magazine.* Retrieved from http://www.nais.org/ Magazines-Newsletters/ISMagazine/Pages/Brainology.aspx

Dweck, Carol S. (2015). "Carol Dweck Revisits the 'Growth Mindset.'" *Education Week.* Retrieved from http://www.edweek.org/ew/articles/2015/09/23/ carol-dweck-revisits-the-growth-mindset.html

Grant, Carl A. and Agosto, Vonzell. (2008). "Teacher Capacity and Social Justice in Teacher Education." *Educational Leadership and Policy Studies Faculty Publications.* Paper 5.

Jensen, Eric (2009). "How poverty affects behavior and academic performance." Chapter 2 of *Teaching with Poverty in Mind: What Being Poor Does to Kids' Brains and What Schools Can Do About It.* Alexandria, Va.: ASCD.

Krasnoff, Basha (2016). *Culturally Responsive Teaching: A Guide to Evidence-Based Practices for Teaching All Students Equitably.* Retrieved from https://educationnorthwest.org/sites/default/files/resources/culturally-responsive-teaching.pdf

Leaf, Caroline (2018). *Think, Learn, Succeed: Understanding and Using Your Mind to Thrive at School, the Workplace, and Life.* Baker Books.

Lopez, S. J., Rose, S., Robinson, C., Marques, S. C., and Pais-Ribeiro, J. (2014). "Measuring and promoting hope in schoolchildren." In M. J. Furlong, R. Gilman, and E. S. Huebner (Eds.), *Handbook of Positive Psychology in Schools, 2nd Edition*. New York: Taylor & Francis.

Lopez, S. J., Snyder, C. R., Magyar-Moe, J. L., Edwards, L. M., Pedrotti, J. T., Janowski, K., . . . Pressgrove, C. (2004). Strategies for Accentuating Hope. In P. A. Linley & S. Joseph (Eds.), *Positive psychology in practice* (pp. 388-404). Hoboken, NJ, US: John Wiley & Sons Inc.

Marques, S. C., Lopez, S. J., and Pais-Ribeiro, J. L. (2009). "'Building Hope for the Future': A Program to foster strengths in middle school students." *Journal of Happiness Studies*. Retrieved from http://www.ofyp.umn.edu/ofypmedia/pdfs/ highered/fye/bhf.pdf

McKnight, Patrick E. and Kashdan, Todd B. (2009). "Purpose in life as a system that creates and sustains health and well-being: An Integrative, testable theory." *Review of General Psychology*, 13(3).

Ng, Betsy (2018). The Neuroscience of Growth Mindset and Intrinsic Motivation. *Brain sciences*, 8(2), 20. doi:10.3390/brainsci8020020

Paunesku, David (2013). "Scaled-up social psychology: Intervening widely and broadly in education." Unpublished dissertation, Department of Psychology, Stanford University. Retrieved from https://web.stanford.edu/~paunesku/articles/paunesku_2013.pdf

Paunesku, D., Walton, G. M., Romero, C., Smith, E. N., Yeager, D. S., and Dweck C. S. (2015). "Mind-set interventions are a scalable treatment for academic underachievement." *Psychological Science*, 26(4).

Sheehan, Kevin and Rall, Kevin (2011). "Rediscovering hope: Building school cultures of hope for children of poverty." *Phi Delta Kappan* 93(3).

Snyder, C. R. (2003). Measuring Hope in Children. Paper presented at the Indicators of Positive Development Conference in Washington, D.C. [Based in part on Snyder et al. (1997) in *Journal of Pediatric Psychology*.] Retrieved from https://www.childtrends.org/wp-content/uploads/2013/05/Child_Trends-2003_03_12_PD_PDConfSnyder.pdf

Snyder, C. R., Rand, Kevin L., and Sigmon, David R. (2018). "Hope Theory": A Member of the Positive Psychology Family" in *The Oxford Handbook of Hope, Second Edition*. Eds. Matthew W. Gallagher & Shane J. Lopez. Oxford University Press.

Snyder, C. R., Shorey, H. S., Cheavens, J., Pulvers, K. M., Adams, V. H., III, and Wiklund, C. (2002). "Hope and academic success in college." *Journal of Educational Psychology*, 94(4).

Yeager, David S. and Bundick, Matthew J. (2009). "The Role of purposeful work goals in promoting meaning in life and in schoolwork during adolescence." *Journal of Adolescent Research*, 24(4).

Yeager, D. S., Paunesku, D., Walton, G., D'Mello, S., Spitzer, B. J., and Duckworth, A. L. (2014). *Boring but Important: A Self-Transcendent Purpose for Learning Fosters Academic Self-Regulation*. Retrieved from https://labs.la.utexas.edu/adrg/files/2013/12/Purpose.pdf

Zimmerman, Barry J. (2000). "Self-efficacy: An Essential motive to learn." *Contemporary Educational Psychology*, 25(1).

Implement mixed ability instruction

Ballantine, J., and Larres, P. M. (2007). "Cooperative learning: A pedagogy to improve students' generic skills." *Education + Training*, 49, 126-137.

Cohen, Elizabeth G., Lotan, Rachel A., Scarloss, Beth A., and Arellano, Adele R. "Equity in Cooperative Learning Classrooms." Retrieved from https://complexinstruction.stanford.edu/about/Equity-in-Cooperative-Learning-Classrooms

Heltemes, Lynzee (2009). "Social and Academic Advantages and Disadvantages of Within-class Heterogeneous and Homogeneous Ability Grouping." Mathematical and Computing Sciences Masters. Paper 93.

"The Jigsaw Classroom." Retrieved from http://www.jigsaw.org/index.html

"Jigsaw Strategy."(2007). Retrieved from https://www.schreyerinstitute.psu.edu/pdf/alex/jigsaw.pdf

Kahlenberg, Richard and Potter, Halley (2015). "A Smarter Charter: City Neighbors." The Century Foundation. Retrieved from https://tcf.org/content/ report/a-smarter-charter-city-neighbors/

Kohli, Sonali and Quartz (2014). Retrieved from https://www.theatlantic.com/education/archive/2014/11/modern-day-segregation-in-public-schools/382846/

Poole, D. (2008). "Interactional Differentiation in the Mixed-Ability Group: A Situated View of Two Struggling Readers." *Reading Research Quarterly*, 43(3).

Potter, Halley (2012). "Integrated Schools, Integrated Classrooms." The Century Foundation. Retrieved from https://tcf.org/content/commentary/integrated-schools-integrated-classrooms/

Program for Complex Instruction. Retrieved from http://cgi.stanford.edu/group/pci/cgi-bin/site.cgi

Saaris, Natalie (2019). "How can students work together in a mixed-ability classroom?" Retrieved from https://www.activelylearn.com/post/collaboration-mixed-ability-classroom

Tomlinson, Carol A. (2014). *The Differentiated Classroom: Responding to the Needs of All Learners, 2nd Edition*. Alexandria, Va.: ASCD.

Tomlinson, Carol A. (2017). *How to Differentiate Instruction in Academically Diverse Classrooms, 3rd Edition*. Alexandria, Va: ASCD.

Give feedback

Center for Innovation in Research and Teaching. "Effective Feedback in the Classroom." Retrieved from https://cirt.gcu.edu/teaching3/tips/effectivefeed

Centre for Enhanced Teaching & Learning. "Feedback that Improves Student Performance." Retrieved from https://www.unbtls.ca/teachingtips/feedbackthatimprovesperformance.html

Frey, Nancy, Fisher, Douglas, and Smith, Dominique (2019). *All Learning is Social and Emotional: Helping Students Develop Essential Skills for the Classroom and Beyond*. Alexandria, Va: ASCD.

Stenger, Marianne (2014). "5 Research-Based Tips for Providing Students with Meaningful Feedback." Retrieved from https://www.edutopia.org/blog/tips-providing-students-meaningful-feedback-marianne-stenger

Wiggins, Grant (2012). "Seven Keys to Effective Feedback." *Educational Leadership*, 70(1).

Offer learning support opportunities

America's Promise Alliance (2016). *Don't Quit on Me: What Young People Who Left School Say About the Power of Relationships*. Retrieved from http:// www.americaspromise.org/sites/default/files/d8/2016-10/FullReport%20 DontQuit_23mar16_0.pdf

Blum, Robert (2005). *School Connectedness: Improving the Lives of Students*. Baltimore, Md.: Johns Hopkins Bloomberg School of Public Health. Retrieved from http://www.jhsph.edu/research/centers-and-institutes/military-childinitiative/resources/MCI_Monograph_FINAL.pdf

Bromberg, Marni and Theokas, Christina (2016). *Meandering Toward Graduation: Transcript Outcomes of High School Graduates*. https://edtrust.org/wp-content/uploads/2014/09/MeanderingTowardGraduation_EdTrust_April2016.pdf

Bruce, Mary and Bridgeland, John (2014). *The Mentoring Effect: Young People's Perspectives on the Outcomes and Availability of Mentoring*. Civic Enterprises in association with Hart Research Associates. Retrieved from http:// www.mentoring.org/images/uploads/Report_TheMentoringEffect.pdf

2015 KIDS COUNT Data Book: State Trends in Child Well-Being. The Annie E. Casey Foundation. Retrieved from http://www.aecf.org/resources/the-2015-kidscount-data-book/

Krasnoff, Basha (2016). *Culturally Responsive Teaching: A Guide to Evidence-Based Practices for Teaching All Students Equitably*. Retrieved from https://educationnorthwest.org/sites/default/files/resources/culturally-responsive-teaching.pdf

Pannoni, Alexandra (2015). "Mentoring programs aim to increase high school graduates." *U.S. News & World Report*. Retrieved from http://www.usnews.com/ education/blogs/high-school-notes/2015/03/23/mentoring-programs-aim-toincrease-high-school-graduates

Zimmerman, Barry J. and Schunk, Dale H. (Eds.) (2009). *Self-Regulated Learning and Academic Achievement: Theoretical Perspectives, 2nd Edition*. New York: Routledge.

Engage families and communities

Center for Great Public Schools (2008). *Parent, Family, Community Involvement in Education: An NEA Policy Brief*. National Education Association. Retrieved from http://www.nea.org/assets/docs/PB11_ParentInvolvement08.pdf

Hammond, Wayne and Zimmerman, Rob. (2012). *A Strengths-Based Perspective*. Retrieved from https://shed-the-light.webs.com/documents/RSL_STRENGTH_BASED_PERSPECTIVE.pdf

The Harvard Family Research Project separated from Harvard University in 2017 to become the Global Family Research Project: https://globalfrp.org/Articles/Welcome-to-the-Global-Family-Research-Project

Krasnoff, Basha (2016). *Culturally Responsive Teaching: A Guide to Evidence-Based Practices for Teaching All Students Equitably*. Retrieved from https://educationnorthwest.org/sites/default/files/resources/culturally-responsive-teaching.pdf

Leithwood, Kenneth (2010). "Characteristics of school districts that are exceptionally effective in closing the achievement gap." *Leadership and Policy in Schools*, 9(3).

Swartz, Mallary I., Bartlett, Jessica D., and Vele-Tabaddor, Elisa (2016). "Strengths-based education and practice" in *The SAGE Encyclopedia of Contemporary Early Childhood Education*. Thousand Oaks: Sage Publications, Inc.

www.ingramcontent.com/pod-product-compliance
Lightning Source LLC
Chambersburg PA
CBHW030236100526
44584CB00015BB/1502